THE LITTLE BOOK
OF NO REGRETS

The
Little
Book
of
No Regrets

A MINDSET REFRESHER FOR THE MENTALLY EXHAUSTED

DR LAKSHINIE GUNASIRI

COPYRIGHT NOTICE

This Content is the copyright of Lakshinie Gunasiri © 2024. All rights reserved. Any redistribution or reproduction of part or all of the Content in any form is prohibited.

You may not share, copy or redistribute this Content in any medium or format at any time. Our Content is for your individual personal use only and may not be used for commercial purposes. You are not permitted to make any derivative material, including but not limited to copying, reproducing, transforming, sharing or building upon the Content in whole or any part thereof. For any other use or distribution, you must have express written consent from Lakshinie Gunasiri.

DISCLAIMER FOR GENERAL HEALTH CONTENT

The information and any recommendations provided in our videos, presentations, webinars, e-books, printed content, online courses, blog, website and all our materials (together 'Content') are based on our own research, experience and views. The information is intended to be general information, covering general health issues and common life. Whilst we try our best to ensure that the information in our Content is accurate, sometimes there may be errors, inaccuracies or new research that has not been included.

We hope you find this information helpful but please be aware that any information, recommendations or comments may not be suitable for your particular circumstances and you should not take anything in our Content as personal advice. The information in our Content is offered in good faith and it is not specific to any one person or any personal circumstances.

For this reason, we cannot be held liable for any decisions you make based on any of our Content, information, recommendations or views. Any decision you take based on information in this Content is done at your own risk and any consequences, as a result, are your own. You shall indemnify this business, its directors and employees for any and all claims, whether resulting directly or indirectly from your actions based on our Content.

ISBN 978-0-646-89756-1 (in print hardcover)
ISBN 978-0-646-89610-6 (in print paperback)

Published by JOEY & CO PUBLISHING Pty Ltd
21 Fourth Avenue
Klemzig, SA, 5087
Australia
First edition: June 2024

Cover design: Tiago Pereira (99designs.com/profiles/pereiratiago)

*To my unnamed friend
whose life was cut short before
finishing medical school.*

Table of Contents

Preface — 9

Introduction — 11

CHAPTER 1
Own your life — 23

CHAPTER 2
Give your life direction — 41

CHAPTER 3
Trust yourself — 79

CHAPTER 4
Live for today — 95

CHAPTER 5
Let nature take over your pain — 119

Afterword — 139

Endnotes — 143

About the Author — 145

Acknowledgments — 147

Preface

The rising sun is bright and bold, generously filling every corner of the room. I'm covered head to toe with the soothing freshness of crisp cotton sheets. My whole body feels relaxed and light – a familiar and sought-after sensation, especially on the weekend. Through half-open blinds, the sun reflects on the mirror, sending a touch of gold to everything it reaches. It's a magical space I never want to leave.

From where I lie, I can see two empty beds in the room down the hallway and a trail of toys on the floor leading to that room. The house is full of calming silence, although I can hear the birds chirping on a tree somewhere out in the garden. Everything appears as it was last night, except for the empty beds and the shadowy patterns on the walls dancing as the wind blows softly, adding an extra touch to the blissfulness of the morning – a reminder of the summer arriving soon.

The calmness is mesmerising and my body is limp, hesitant to move, seated up on the bed. Yet my mind is already preparing to welcome the day, awakened by the invasion and the giggles that took place seconds ago. My laptop had a near-miss as it toppled off my lap. I wouldn't say I am enjoying this sudden change of events.

After a stretch and a yawn, my eyes rest on two heads that pop up from underneath the blanket on either side of me. One has messy curls with a touch of brown; the other, straight hair, softer, stark black. Amused by the scene, I can't stop laughing, and two sets of eyes stare at me, pretending to be unhappy.

'Mommy, is this a chapter book?'

Excited as always, Senuki peeps into the screen, her curious hands exploring the skin on my arms while she talks, her little fingers tickling me.

'Yes,' I answer, as I try to escape the tickle.

'What about?'

'It's about how to live a beautiful and exciting life, Senuki.'

Her face lights up, and her eyes widen with surprise as she looks at me with a wide grin, showing her snow-white little teeth. She had a charming smile even when she was little. I remember the midwife admiring her beauty at her six-week check-up after the birth.

As I start to read the book out loud, Nisini, my youngest, listens quietly, watching my face, her beautiful eyes overflowing with love.

How different can twins be? I wonder, as I scroll down the page and read to them.

Introduction

A gust of cold air hit my face as the clinic door swung open. I stepped out into the settling darkness, wrapping my winter coat around me, and felt the fabric's big, warm hug. As I dug deep into my pocket to find my keys, I walked carefully to avoid slipping on the wet paving. While ticking off my to-do list for the day one last time in my head, I put my foot on the accelerator of my 2011 Toyota, saving me from the list of things still to be done. Headlights flashed against the darkness and the row of cars inched forward as if the cold weather was making everyone slow. The gloominess and dampness went hand in hand with the turmoil in my mind.

As the music flowed from the car stereo, I was transported to the land of dreams – and there were plenty of those for me to linger on. Settling into my car-seat cocoon and embracing its warmth, I sighed deeply, relieving the tightness in my chest.

When I reach the end of a drive, I feel sad because it stops my silent exploration of the surroundings along the way. I explore with my eyes and mentally note what I see. I always enjoyed that, even as a child; it's the reason I love travelling. An archway of roses, an entryway with wide double doors, an inviting name post with a letterbox on top, a well-kept lawn and a tall gum tree at the far end of the garden. This goes on and on until I stop wherever I want to stop.

Driving through familiar landscapes with an ever-growing curiosity, I was part of the city's workforce rushing home to greet their loved ones. My heart was heavy, and I moved in my seat to see if I could reduce its weight.

Suddenly, my head turned to the side as if by magic, and I felt a new vibe. My heart skipped a beat, as always when I was in this spot. I found myself looking at the property to my left.

It was right next to the traffic lights, offering my wandering eyes a treat as I travelled down the road. As always, I wondered who lived there and what type of house it was, as I could not see much with the climbing plants covering the walls. The garden was poorly kept, but it looked occupied. It was on a corner, bordered by the road on both sides, with well-established trees along the road. The branches of the trees met in the middle, making a natural archway that flared up in blazing yellow, red and orange in autumn. I took a deep breath and felt goosebumps on my skin and blood rushing through my veins.

I could not stop my imagination from taking over. In my mind, it was now a warm summer evening …

The large two-storey house stood proudly at the end of the long driveway, with a water fountain in front of the main entrance, its tinkling water welcoming visitors to the home. The fragrance of roses and lavender along the driveway created a sense of nostalgia, and the purple and pink blossoms moved gently in the warm breeze. Beyond the two-door entrance was a high ceiling with a large chandelier showering its light like stars from heaven to earth, sending a clear message: 'It's finally yours.'

Beyond the warm and spacious lounge, the entryway to the left

Introduction

led to a large dining area with a table set for dinner – the French croissants and soup caught my hungry eye.

A warm summer breeze entered through the open window. Through the pane, in the far distance, I could see the skyscrapers of Melbourne illuminated softly against the setting sun, which was colouring the sky in shades of pink and grey.

The aroma of the warm soup and fresh lavender made my knees wobble, and I felt even hungrier. I sank into a plush chair to join my family to enjoy the feast. Amidst the conversation and laughter, I imagined a good sleep after dinner while others spoke enthusiastically about the upcoming Australian Open and other sports.

Then reality hit. I had arrived home.

I could still smell the lavender as I exited my car and hurried inside to escape the shivering cold. While I slumped onto a couch scribbled with crayons, I realised I had no more energy to spend. I was physically exhausted and emotionally drained. I didn't even want to think of anything. Feeling hungry and tired, I wished someone would hand me a bowl of the delicious soup I had imagined seconds ago.

I wondered where it had all gone wrong.

Tears began welling up in my eyes as my spine prickled with fear. I was scared for my future. My life was not how it was meant to be; in fact, it felt like the opposite of how I wanted it to be, and I did not know how to make it right.

A scene from a couple of years ago flashed across my mind.

It was a sunny morning, and I was driving home after a night shift. I was looking forward to this drive in the morning sun. I'd had breakfast with coffee before leaving the hospital and grabbed a bottle of orange juice to take with me to sip while driving. The window was open so the morning air would tickle my face. Feeling relaxed that the shift had ended and my handover had gone successfully, I took off, while contemplating what could have made my practice at the hospital even better. It was the end of four night shifts in a row, and I was excited to have the next four days off. The next thing I knew, I was suddenly awakening – to find myself veering across lanes and heading towards the side of the road at 100 kilometres per hour. I had no idea I had fallen asleep. I was suddenly grateful for being alive, and as I arrived home, I was trembling with fear for my kids, who had yet to learn to walk.

I wondered what would have happened to them if I had died that day.

I always enjoyed my work, the adrenaline rush of saving lives in crisis. I still remember the sixteen packs of blood I prepared for the woman bleeding in theatre and how she walked home later, carrying her baby in her arms. She had cardiac arrested twice on the theatre table and had an aorta flat like a ribbon, which was what the surgeons reported afterwards. Our entire team had been summoned to come to the hospital that night. Another time, a terrified newborn baby had locked her eyes with mine and then closed them again as I took over to save her life; her frightened eyes looked directly into mine as she struggling to breathe with lungs full of meconium. I had never had a baby look so sharply at me; maybe it was the moment she realised she needed help. On another occasion, a newborn had been declared officially dead due to hypothermia before I saved her. Her brain survived, which meant she would be able to walk and talk; it was as if a miracle had happened.

Introduction

Obstetricians cheer as I enter the theatre, and babies cry and breathe along with their happy parents trembling with excitement and hope...

After a row of ten nights in the hospital, my husband was so pleased to see me, he almost wet his pants ... we were newlyweds then. One Monday, my hands trembled so much with hunger, I could not hold the spoon after an 80-hour shift over a weekend. It was an experience I will never forget. I was yelling and screaming, hungry and tired. My battle with sleep deprivation and shift work was unbearable at that time.

When I was about ten, I published an article in a children's newspaper about wanting to be a doctor. My mother still carries that piece of paper with pride. At that age, I thought I would have a big house and a car and wear high heels to work. When I was a teenager, lots of my friends were excited about their boyfriends, while I was excited about the chemistry and botany I was being taught. I was known for my good looks, and had more than a few admirers, some secret and some public. But sadly, for them, I was admiring medical school more than the boys. When I was in medical school, some people even suggested I would get endometriosis before I had babies because I was too selective about who I chose to be with and would therefore be very late to marry!

Just as I have a curious eye when I travel and look around me, I have a curious inner eye for life experiences. I enjoy exploring life with my mind's eye.

When I was in my first year of medical school, mental illnesses were not uncommon among my colleagues. It was thought that every new intake would have one person with schizophrenia and they would not finish medical training – and it appeared it was true at the time as I watched some of them struggle. I remember being very anxious myself. Competition and coping with stress are not everyone's cup of tea.

In time, I realised people liked talking to me about their problems, and I was good at helping them find solutions. For my family, I was a saviour, a hero and a role model academically. Their expectations of me were high – in my career and everything else. I helped cement my family's excellent reputation in academic success. But for me, I was just another confused young person scared for the future. I worried about my future and the dreams I had. I wouldn't deny enjoying being the family saviour, though. I tried my best to make everyone happy, and I was continuously in trouble for doing that, I realise now. It is not a good idea for anyone to take responsibility for making everyone else happy at the expense of your own happiness.

I learned from what I observed and experienced as I moved through medical school and life. Learning from mistakes was good, but some mistakes hurt beyond imagination. Watching how some people regret what they did made me sad and made me rethink what I did. As I listened and observed, some regretted their career choice, their choice of a life partner, and which campus they joined to learn medicine. I heard some regretting their decision to marry, and some even regretting having children. I observed how they suffered, how their relationships had ups and downs, and how marriages fell apart. I also regretted some of my own decisions about my relationships, too.

For me, life was a straight line. I thought you started from one point and reached the other, straight and no detours, please. It was do or die. Regrets indicated a bad choice somewhere. I wasn't going to waste my time on bad choices – I wanted to make the choice that worked for me and do my happily-ever-after life with everything happening in my favour. I wanted to create a life without regrets to avoid painful mistakes.

That is how my journey of a life without regrets came about. But then what happened?

I had my eyes set on a life that would serve me as the person I was. I wanted fun, variety, personal growth, money and to serve big. I wanted it all and did not want to give up one thing for another. I was very confident in that, as I was good at achieving whatever I wanted; I always had a knack for that.

But as I went on, I realised I had an internal struggle going on – a struggle about choices. This struggle manifested as a never-ending spiral of thoughts in my head. Something felt wrong in my head. It felt like I had taken a wrong turn, but I could not determine what it was.

I wanted the right partner who I could stick with for life.

I wanted a happy marriage and an advancing career. Many people believe a woman can't have both, especially growing up in a third-world country like I did. I observed many strong-willed women who inspired me, and the struggles they had trying to do both.

I wanted kids and a growing income. People say kids suck your money and steal your time in terms of financial and career growth.

I wanted personal time and many responsibilities.

I wanted to be well known for doing something good for humanity but also to be the introvert I tended to be.

I was confused about whether I was actually an introvert – because while I could feel content being alone in a crowded room, I also secretly dreamed of speaking publicly to inspire others.

I wanted it all, but how could I have it all simultaneously and make the correct choices every time so that I would be successful? Sometimes I was immobilised by fear of making the wrong choice. I wanted a guarantee that my choices would be right.

My goals were never-ending, and I was on a journey going from one achievement to another. The more goals I had, the more choices I had to make. I was exhausted from my unlimited dreams for life, yet I didn't want to give up. I've never known what giving up is like – *never done that* – and that was the secret behind me being the hero achiever.

I regretted many of my life choices daily. How come a life I had planned to ensure no regrets was giving me more and more regrets?

Mommy!

I was instantly back in the here and now on the crayon-covered couch at home. Two little bodies were crawling into my lap. I realised they could read my mind even at that tender age. Smart little cookies! I kissed their little heads gently; the softness and the smell of their hair helped soothe my mind. I looked around – voices in the distance told me my husband was still occupied with his work.

What was it that was not right with this life? I'd achieved status, responsibilities, money – and regrets! Regrets were part of my daily life, and they made me very confused.

This level of physical exhaustion was certainly not something I

Introduction

had expected ... emotional strain and overwork led to lack of connections ... financial insecurity was keeping me up at night. Most of all, I felt like this was not *my* life I was living – and that was unbearable. My old habit of always putting others ahead of me was having its toll on me.

Was I to accept all this as the life I wanted? Never, I thought. Not unless I die tonight.

What on earth was I supposed to do to make this life right?

And then a realisation hit me on the head. I realised I needed to change the direction of my life. That realisation changed my life forever.

How could I aim for a life without regrets – and expect not to have regrets? Why didn't I realise this before? I was so shocked my whole body felt numb.

A slight smile made its way onto my lips. I rocked back and forth, still holding the two little people on my lap. The smile on my lips stretched into a grin as I bit my lip with the understanding that I had finally found the root of the problem. I almost danced with joy and cried happy tears.

I have no words to tell you how light my heart felt; I could almost fly.

A few more realisations crept into my brain in that blissful moment.

I was still waiting for others to make me happy.

I was still waiting for others to approve of me.

I was holding myself back with the fear of the unknown.

I was still not controlling my life – but I was complaining.

I realised I had settled for a much smaller life all these years – the real life I aimed for was much bigger. All I needed to do was let loose the restraints I had on my mind and stop seeking the approval of others to do what I liked.

I was holding back what I wanted to do with my life, waiting for the perfect moment to start – and I knew the perfect moment was now.

All this time, I had been looking around for others for inspiration, and all I saw was how some people served the world and lived beyond imagination while living luxurious lives, and others, like me, suffered trying to do the same thing. I had wondered where and how to tweak, and now I knew.

I had been living small, thinking small, running away from everything I wanted to have out of fear.

I decided that very moment to live the life I always wanted. There was no turning back now, good doctor!

I started writing this book you are reading soon after. I focused on the projects I had always wanted to do. I deliberately did things to create happy moments with my family. I made sure I exercised and ate healthy. I did things exactly as I wanted things to be – no matter how small or big. I took steps to create financial freedom and security.

I allowed myself to do what I wanted to do with no permission from anyone.

A few months later, one of my biggest problems had been solved. I suddenly found I had so much more time for everything I wanted to do. Can you believe that? If I found the time, anyone can find the time!

You have enough time to do anything when you do what you

Introduction

want. Period.

Even if I die tonight, I have now done everything I wanted to do and lived the way I wanted to live. No regrets.

How come?

Is this a scam or some fairy tale?

No.

I only changed one thing: I switched from living without regrets to living the beautiful and exciting life I wanted. I changed the direction of my life from running away from what I did not want to living exactly how I always wanted.

How do you stop running away from what you don't want?

Well, keep reading to find out.

Own your life

See through the patterns to find the real you.

In my third year of medical school in Sri Lanka, I started working towards living without regrets. This helped me make important decisions differently, add a new perspective and rethink my actions. When I made this decision, I was influenced by some of my life experiences and those of other people close to me.

If you are reading this book, you are also looking for a life without regrets, just as I was.

I follow a fundamental principle: it has helped me transform my life into one without regrets, i.e. my beautiful and exciting life. I didn't invent this principle so anyone can use it and test it out.

It just shows the reality of the world. Whether or not you accept it, this principle remains constant and does not change over time or across generations. This is a crucial and fundamental concept in personal development. You are free to deny what I'm about to tell you, but you cannot change it. That is just the nature of it and the world.

If you are not happy with the life you are living, how would you feel if I told you that you created your life, and hence you are responsible for your own mess?

Irritated? I'm not surprised.

Do you mean that agonising boss who dumps all her dirty work on my desk so I have no time to be with my kids is my fault, Lakshinie?

I can almost hear you saying it! But there is more to come; don't throw away the book yet ...

As much as it can be unpleasant to hear, it can be the opposite, too. For me, understanding this concept was a blessing. If you understand that, you have a magic wand that allows you to tap and change anything. Period.

In the world of personal development, it is well-known that a person is responsible for their own life. Accepting responsibility allows a person to change their life, as they can then change the actions that have produced the experiences needing to be modified.

When you understand you are responsible for your own experiences and accept that, and operate from that acceptance, you take control of your life and stop allowing other people to make the decisions that drive your life.

In other words, when you accept responsibility for your life and what you experience, you take your life back into your own hands. That is how you own your life.

So, if that boss is still dumping her dirty work on your table, there are things you can do to change it forever. How does that sound, my friend?

When you operate from accepting your experiences as your responsibility, you have the freedom to choose what you want to experience. Isn't that wonderful?

It also makes you understand the unlimited possibilities you have. The other benefit of taking responsibility for your own life is that you learn that nothing in life is concrete, and you are free to change anything as long as you are ready to accept the changes you make and their consequences.

We all have problems accepting the changes other people want us to make. That discomfort of accepting another person's influence in life is also related to the fact that no one else can change our lives.

When you accept responsibility for your own life and understand that only *you* can make changes to it, you understand that if anyone else is to make changes to your life, you need to agree with the change they are proposing and take action accordingly.

If you feel other people are driving your life, that is because you have agreed with the other person at some level and incorporated their viewpoint into yours. You are still the action-taker. If you do not want other people driving your life, you need to be aware of your thinking process and the actions that will follow.

When you accept and operate from the understanding that whatever you do results in your experiences, you stop blaming others for your problems. Instead, you look at problems to find where you can tweak them to change their impact on you. If you can create a certain experience for yourself, you can always *uncreate* or *change* the experience, too.

I do not mean you should break the law – you can still change experiences within the moral standards of where you live. Otherwise, you will be struggling to change unpleasant experiences, some of which may be irreversible such as being in trouble with law and going to jail.

You may initially have difficulty accepting this principle, but whether or not you accept it, it still exists. The longer it takes to understand it, the longer it will take to change the things that impact you in a way you don't like. What you can do until you fully understand this concept is to think about your life and any particular situations you would like to change.

No one else can change how you intend to live unless you allow them to. Allowing others to decide for you is your choice. You always have the option to change this situation.

Understanding that no one else can change my destiny has helped me get rid of the fear of the unknown. Initially, I believed it out of despair. But my beliefs were consolidated as I witnessed the effects believing it had on my actions and the results I witnessed in my life. Later, I understood the concept in more in-depth as I delved further into personal development. With a deepened understanding, I trusted that no one else could change my life and accepted that as a reality wholeheartedly.

Let me tell you a story.

When I was at medical school, I was extremely unhappy. Someone there bullied me almost every day. The bully would verbally abuse me and make vulgar comments about me in public. I was scared people would believe his lies were true and worried about the damage it would have on my reputation and future. It was awful to be in a medical school and have this happen, as my expectations of budding doctors were rather different to what I was experiencing. Because of the class arrangements, I could not avoid this person who I encountered almost daily. I was also concerned about changing my study group; I thought if I did, it would make others see me as a misfit. It continued for a long time and began affecting me in various ways. I cried every day. I feared the bully and thinking about the future scared me. This experience changed how I perceived my life at medical school and made me realise that my expectations of my colleagues were unrealistic. I lacked the skills to handle the frustration and emotional pain. I was a go-getter; I only knew how to achieve and be a winner, not how to accept frustration and move on. My attitude was straight-line 'do or die'. But I did not want to die either.

Dealing with emotional pain is a life skill that can help anyone, but how do you do that without seeking suicide?

The bully made me so scared for my future I couldn't stop thinking about what could happen if the situation continued. I was so worried I would go home in the evening, cry and complain about everything and everyone. I felt scared by the slightest thing. I was in an overwhelmingly anxious state that stopped me from looking ahead in my life. I started to live without much excitement for the future. Fear was engulfing my life. The bully's words were echoing in my ears all the time. Focusing on things that mattered to me was hard, and nothing would calm me down.

When I lost focus on my work, I lost my secret weapon in life. My purpose came from focusing on what I was doing. And because I was so focused, I wasn't bothered by what others thought of me, and I could shut down any negativity. But unfortunately, the bully was able to unseat all of that – and without my arrow-like focus, I suddenly cared what others thought of me. My head was full of fearful thoughts, and I desperately sought a solution.

I discovered a place that offered free professional counselling services for young people. I'm so thankful such a place existed. Although the staff were not highly skilled, they provided compassionate listening. I could go there any time to cry before a stranger until my heart had had enough. But that was not what I wanted. I wanted to learn not to cry and how to move on when things didn't go as planned. I wanted to heal my emotional pain, silence the fearful chatter that went on in my head, and learn how to stop being regretful. I was desperate to get my thoughts right. Just crying in front of someone and getting the agony out of my heart verbally did not have lasting effects.

Ultimately, the person who helped me make a change was my mother – as always. My mother comes from a Buddhist background and is very religious. We often argue about why I'm not religious like her. I always thought learning religion and doing religious rituals were two different things. Therefore, I believed in learning new concepts rather than blindly following a religion.

When she heard about what I was going through, she took me to meet a monk she thought could help me by redirecting my thinking, even though she was concerned about the confidentiality of the matter. I think she was also trying to get me on board with her view of practising religion and engaging with rituals – that was the solution she could offer with what she knew.

The monk was a famous intellect with a good reputation in Buddhist societies. He had a very pleasant but fragile demeanour. I still remember his kind face, how he talked to me and what he said. Although he was fragile in his health, he appeared to be coping with his disability amazingly well. He had problems speaking because of his health situation, so he used an electronic device that caught his voice and transmitted it to others to hear – a very sensitive mini-microphone. But his wisdom was certainly not fragile, like his voice was. What he emphasised for me was very simple. He said that no one could ever change my destiny other than myself and that I had a lot of potential to succeed. He emphasised again that no one could ever take my future away from me.

That was all I wanted to hear – that my future was safe and no one could change it. I didn't understand what it meant that no one could change my life, though; I just saw it as a motivational thought that gave me courage. And courage was what I needed.

Thinking about what the monk had said was soothing to my burning emotions. To distract my fearful mind, I visualised my meeting with the monk and repeated his words quietly in my head regularly, so much so that even when I woke up in the middle of the night, I heard those words echoing in my head. It served as an affirmation. As time passed, the monk's words echoed in my ears, replacing the bully. After some time, my internal distress started disappearing. I found a new energy and trust in myself. Although my relationship with the bully never recovered and my social life was messy, I could focus better. The bully carried on his bullying, and I carried on with my life, looking forward to the day I would finish medical school. Life continued with redirections and detours; it was never a straight line after medical school. I could say I was in pursuit of happiness, a pursuit of no regrets.

A few years later, I had moved to Australia to live, gotten married and was starting a family. I was hopeful for a beautiful future again and started planning for such. But then, I found myself facing a challenging situation in my career. I met with a roadblock that stopped me from stepping into the future I was creating as a paediatrician. This challenge had a different depth and meaning to me as I was much older and had other responsibilities and commitments I could not escape. By then, thankfully, I already knew I had to make internal changes to overcome the challenge.

But how?

Coincidentally, I had signed up for a life-coaching workshop, where I learned another important lesson. One concept explained during the workshop was that no one can change another person; we can only change ourselves. I already knew that, but listening to it from a professional life coach was interesting.

I didn't know the other concept: that a challenge exists because you are capable of resolving the issue and overcoming the challenge.

'If there is a problem or challenge you are facing right now, it is because now you have the capacity to resolve the issue and overcome the situation,' the instructor went on.

I sat there, soaking up all I was hearing. It was just what I needed to hear! If I had not been there that day and had not heard that, I'm not sure how my life would be right now.

Isn't it a wonderful thing that if a challenge presents itself, you have the capacity to resolve the challenge yourself?

I was so relieved driving home that day – I felt like floating on air.

Isn't it wonderful to know that no one else can change your life, and that you can find a solution to any problem you face just by working on yourself?

Own your life

It makes life much simpler knowing this. You only need to deal with one person your whole life – that is yourself.

As I understood this concept, I saw the patterns I had experienced in my life. Some patterns put me at an advantage over others. Some patterns made me helpless and miserable.

Bullying was nothing new to me.

People always ask me what my name means. My mother gave me the name, with its implied meaning of wealth. But interestingly, my name could also be tweaked to mean 'evil person' in Sinhalese. You just need to replace the letter 'L' in the beginning with a 'Y', and then it means something completely different.

Did I like my name?

No. Not a bit.

When I was in primary school, I felt as if I was a target. A gang of children in my class would call me names, spit on my desk, and do other things to irritate me. Which seven-year-old would like to be called evil by her friends? I despised my mother's wisdom for giving me this name. My mother boldly suggested I change my name when I complained, but would you have done that when you were just seven? To me, that was scary. Would you name your child and then tell them to change it later if they didn't like it? 'That's crazy' was all I could think.

I thought the bullies were jealous of me, which is what my mother always told me. She believed I was destined to attract jealous people, for some weird reason, and liked rambling about it regularly, so I was well aware of it. But that kind of thinking did not offer an escape or a way to change the situation. What helped me undo the pattern many years later was reflecting on what *I did* at that time.

What did I do? I went home and complained to my mother, as always – but surprisingly, not to the class teacher, who could have controlled the situation. Why? My class teacher and I were close and I could have told her anything.

Why didn't I do what would give me the desired result instead of choosing something that did not help me?

I now realise I agreed with the bullies unconsciously, so I did not want to change the situation. What I wanted to change was something else. I believed the bullies were doing the right thing. The bullies would distort my name and call it out aloud in class, at recess and at other times! I did not like my name either. Why would I change something when I believed it was right? I could have seen their actions differently if I had not believed the bullies were right. I was an excellent student, and they were having a go at the best student in class in order to feel superior. It made them feel good, while I had found others who agreed with my beliefs. I unconsciously knew the bullies were saying the right thing – that my name was a bad choice.

The bullies caught me in a spot where I was in pain. The bullies did not create the pain; instead, they pointed out where I was hurting.

The bullies were helpless and did what they knew to overcome their helplessness.

I was helpless, and I did what I thought was best for the situation – I found an excuse to show my mother her poor choice of name. The bullies gave me the excuse I was looking for. With the bullies' help, I found what I sought – a way to resolve my problem.

Had there been bullying at all? The bullies had done me a favour.

Both the bullies and I took the right action unconsciously, although, at a conscious level, it did not make sense. We both wanted to resolve a problem. The bullies wanted to feel better. I wanted to voice my opinion. What's wrong with that?

The bullies were insecure, and I was insecure, too. We just crashed into each other and found a situation that helped each of us to overcome our insecurity. What was wrong was how we did what we did to overcome the insecurity. The intentions were good, but the actions reflected a different intention underneath the undesirable behaviour.

Similarly, at medical school, the bully there caught me with his verbal abuse when I felt insecure about my life and was badly criticising myself internally. The problem existed before the bully showed up in my life. My life situation was such that I needed to re-learn and be reassured that I could have the life I always wanted. I needed to stop the self-blame that was going on in my head. I needed to get my thinking process right. The bully indirectly helped me resolve an internal conflict.

It was my messy head, attracting another mess. There is a saying that birds of a feather flock together, right?

The bully was helpless, and I acted helpless, too. The bully went on making himself feel good, being the hero to make someone else look small. It would have been a good service to myself and the bully if I could see him for who he was and the insecurity that was driving his pathetic behaviour. I was hurting already. But I began my journey to heal myself, driven by this incident, thanks to the bully.

It was the blessing I needed; I wouldn't have survived medical school without learning what I learned.

But could I have learned that lesson any other way?

It makes little sense that I am bullied everywhere because there are so many bullies; instead, there must be something within me that attracts all that bullying. That something was a specific pattern of thinking leading to a specific pattern of behaviour, consolidating into certain habits as I went on, which made me attract bullies.

When you see patterns of experiences arising from unresourceful thinking and behaviour, you can get rid of them, but only if you believe you are responsible for the life you are living.

If you believe other people can change your life and are responsible for the life you experience, you have no hope of changing your life since that's what you believe is the truth, although it is far from reality.

Your thoughts show up as actions because actions arise from thoughts. Every action arises from a thought, even though you sometimes don't realise the thought has occurred, because of habitual thinking and how quickly you take actions out of habit. Consider the simple act of brushing your teeth. You cannot do it unless you think of it first. Habitually, your hand may move toward where your toothbrush is. But If you forget to think of brushing your teeth, your hand may move elsewhere instead of reaching for the toothbrush. This shows how thoughts precede actions, even though the time between the thought and the action is just a fraction of a second.

Thoughts arise before you act on the thought. Actions create a series of experiences, and collectively, these experiences are called life.

If you want a different life, you need different experiences. To change your experiences, you need to act differently from what you do now. And this begins with different thoughts.

Changing your thoughts changes your life.

If you want a beautiful and exciting life, you need to think of ways to give you beautiful and exciting experiences. Then, your thoughts will become aligned with your desires, which will, in turn, give you the life you want.

Other people cannot access your brain and thoughts unless you share them with others. Similarly, you cannot know what is happening in another person's mind unless they tell you about it.

Have you ever felt that you could never know another person fully, even if they are close to you and you know all their secrets? That is right. You never know others. Do you know yourself fully and one hundred per cent? Have you ever felt that sometimes you even surprise yourself with what you do and think? That means you do not know yourself one hundred per cent, either.

If you don't know how to predict yourself fully, can you fully predict another?

To elaborate, I would like you to think of a red rose. It is highly probable that you just formed a mental image of a red rose in your mind. I also had a picture of a red rose popping up in my head as I asked you to do so. But it's highly unlikely that we both have the same mental image when we think of a red rose. We may both imagine a flower with a similar overall appearance, but the details can vary greatly. When I visualise a red rose, I see a flower with velvety red petals attached to a stalk with thorns and green leaves with tiny, sharp, spiky edges. This symbolises a red rose for me. The thought makes me remember the rich fragrance I have associated with a rose. This mental image reminds me of my wedding when I carried a beautiful bouquet of red roses.

When I was younger, I learned about colours and how red relates to a specific wavelength of the light spectrum. Similarly, over time, I've learned how to identify different varieties of flowers and what makes roses unique. Because of my previous learning, I can identify a rose and label it as such to explain what I see. Because of my previous experiences, I have mentally associated a certain set of memories with roses that represent happiness and romance. Therefore, I get happy and romantic thoughts when I think of a rose.

What is your experience with red roses? Is it the same as mine? If no one taught you what a red rose was, how would you label it the first time you saw it? What thoughts and feelings would it evoke if you had never seen a rose?

Imagine a newborn who sees a red rose for the first time. How do they know what it is and what it represents? How would they label it with no one telling them what a red rose is? While they can see the physical structure of the rose, they do not have the same emotional response as someone who associates red roses with happiness or sadness. The newborn would look at the red rose with curiosity, trying to figure out what this new object is.

The red rose still exists, irrespective of how people perceive it differently. Newborns lack the mental frames that we use to describe objects and experiences. We use pre-learned labels and frames to describe something new, but a newborn does not have that prelearning, nor the labels or frames. Similarly, a colour-blind person's perception of a red rose would differ from someone who can see all the colours. If we consider an alien's perspective, the concept of a red rose would be entirely new to them. They would have to develop their frames of reference to understand what it is and how to label it. They couldn't put a label on it without making an association with another structure they know.

Without pre-learned labels and frames, describing or relating to what is around us is impossible. That means our perception is based on what we already know, influencing our understanding of a situation and our following actions.

What you perceive is a projection of your inner self and what you already know. Your unconscious mind takes the pathway of least resistance in informing you of what you need to know. It makes associations for you, deletes some information, distorts them, and presents them to you in a way that is convenient for you to understand in a way that feels safe to you.

How can people know each other completely if two people don't share the same perception? Two people never share the same interpretation of the external world because what they understand as the external world reflects their own internal world.

If you don't know what is happening in another person's internal representation of their world, how can you change who they are? You cannot do that; if you cannot, no one can do it for you either.

You are safe in your world; the only person who you can change is yourself.

Finding underlying patterns in your life is key to unlocking the information you need to work with to gain control of your life. These patterns may show where you have problems or what you are good at.

If you have a pattern of similar experiences repeating themselves, creating challenges for you, please understand that your unconscious mind is sending you a message by repeatedly showing you the same challenge. You have been invited to find a solution to the problem that is within your reach.

The bullying incidences that repeated in my life occurred because I had a pattern of thinking and behaviour that made me attract bullies. I believed I got bullied easily. With that belief, I created a lower resistance to experiences that are labelled 'bullying'. If I had believed otherwise, I could have had a different life experience from what I have today.

Similarly, I have repeatedly achieved career success despite challenges and distractions. I had a pattern of thinking and behaviour that led me to be successful amidst challenges. My life would have been very different if I did not have that skill. I always believed that I would reach my goals no matter what. To me, failure is not an option and does not exist. At the same time, it shows me my other belief: that success comes through hard work. With that belief, I created obstacles in everything I did. If I had believed success was easy, I would have done the same things more easily and created different life experiences.

What themes or experiences appear repeatedly in your life? Why do you think they occur?

YOUR LIFE WORK

Reflect on your life experiences and identify what similar themes repeat in your life that create problems for you. In the space below, write at least one that creates problems for you and why you think it is repeated.

For your convenience, I have pre-written some of the words in the sentences for one of them. You need to fill in the blanks.

I have experienced incidences of _____ _____ repeating in my life. I have a pattern of thinking and behaviour that leads me to attract _____ _____ _____.

2

Give your life direction

*If you do not give your life a direction to flow,
life will choose a direction for you.*

When I was 19, I secured my entry to medical school. As expected, I passed my advanced-level exam at school with flying colours and felt victorious. I was all set for success in life. I had worked on passing the exam and getting into medical school for the last few years, so I felt confident in myself – I knew how to set a goal and achieve it.

But something interesting happened afterwards. I decided I needed a rest from goal setting. Goal setting was nothing new; I had always used strategic planning in my academic success. As a young person, that is all I had to plan for myself because my parents took care of everything else for me, as is the case for most of us at that age.

My goal-setting method was to visualise and condition myself for success. I did this work secretly to enhance my mindset, although I was unaware of the importance of what I was doing. I had been visualising and conditioning myself for success from a young age. The terms 'visualising' and 'conditioning myself for success' are nothing new to me now, but they were unheard of for a Sri Lankan teenager in the 1980s, so it *was* a secret then. I think I read about right mindset somewhere when I was younger and found it interesting, so I started applying the practice. I'd heard others say that if you make wishes before you fall asleep, God will grant them. So, I made sure God knew my desires, and I later found them being granted exactly as I had wished when I visualised my future as a doctor.

I did that regularly at night while waiting for sleep to arrive, so bedtime was a much-anticipated, fun-filled time for me. That is where I liberated all my fantasies for a beautiful future without needing anyone's permission. I grew up in a family where there was only one choice: to follow directions. But the freedom to choose was never restricted in my bedtime fantasy world. I gave myself the freedom to choose my future – the freedom I did not have during the daytime. Despite many challenges with finances and social circumstances, I was in flow, securing a spot in the faculty of Medicine at the University of Colombo, Sri Lanka. Some thought it would be impossible with all the other challenges in my life. But I was set for success in a medical career in the most prestigious medical school in the country.

Yet somehow, feeling like I had to be pursuing something all the time was exhausting – I was tired of the constant pursuit. I decided to have a more relaxed time and let myself be free of pursuing success, hoping I would feel rejuvenated. So, I stopped visualising my future and decided I would return to goal setting later.

I realised the mistake I had made a few years later when I was feeling miserable because I was getting bullied every day and feeling lost. What was bothering me more was the alarming feeling that I was somehow responsible for this mess. I wondered why I felt I had taken a wrong turn inside my head.

I realised I needed to return to goal setting, but my life was not the same anymore. I was sad and angry, and I regretted what I had done by not setting goals and conditioning myself. I was angry with myself for letting myself down. The ability to forgive myself was not there in my skill set in those days.

Where to from here? I wondered. It's a good thing to wonder, especially if you have no idea what to do next.

I secretly wished I could go back to my teenage self, who knew what she wanted and made sure she achieved it. That teenager, an innocent girl who would say 'yes' to anything and to anyone, deep inside was a daredevil with no fear; she knew how to get her wishes fulfilled even under the most discouraging circumstances.

I decided to pick up where I had left off and began thinking about a life without regrets. Regrets were common in my life in those days, and I really wanted a life without them.

A life without regrets – that everything would happen the way I imagined it, just as it had when I passed my exam and got into medical school. That became my goal. I was excited and in anticipation again. Finally, I could breathe, knowing I would be okay. I started dreaming again, but this time for much bigger dreams. But I had a problem.

I had no consistency.

I was looking for answers to many problems and wasn't sure which problem to sort out first.

I needed to pay attention to my academic success. I had to work on my relationships. I was looking for a partner to create a lasting bond with. I was thinking of post-graduate studies. I planned on creating a career where I could serve others.

Which one should I start with?

I found myself confused; one day, I would visualise academic success; the next day, I focused on my personal life and future partner; followed by nothing for a few days until something bad happened to remind me to go back to goal setting again.

I was confused. I realised I had no genuine passion for any of these things – at least not enough to make me think of them with enthusiasm. I wondered why. I was truly in love with the medical profession and being a doctor; I always told people I would still choose it if I had a second chance to redo my life. So, I prioritised my studies and completed my medical career as an undergraduate. I started serving people and enjoyed how I changed lives as a junior doctor.

I was the saviour. I enjoyed serving and saving lives. But my life was not cruising along as I wanted it to. There were always obstacles and feelings of confusion and being overwhelmed.

I realised I had a problem. I wanted so much, but I struggled with my choices. How would I tie all these dreams together to form one thing I could be, so I didn't have to sacrifice one thing for another?

I had so many dreams and plans, I did not know where to begin. I wanted it all simultaneously and successfully. I was looking for inspiration; I saw people doing one thing after another or sacrificing one thing for another. To excel in a career *and* have a happy marriage was considered unachievable, especially if you were a female.

Some people believed career women were less attractive in the marriage market, as they could outshine their male partners and be too outspoken because of their education and knowledge, which could cause problems in the relationship. Shift work was considered unhealthy for marriage unless you married another doctor – and I must say, I felt I would be bored if I married another doctor. Too much medicine in the house! Some variety would be nice.

People told me success would mean no family time, less sleep, an unhealthy lifestyle and stress, and I could see this for myself as I looked around.

I wanted to marry and have kids when I was still young. I wanted a career and a happy home to return to in the evenings. I loved saving lives – which invariably meant doing night shifts at the hospital. I didn't think I would ever outshine anyone, but I didn't want to hide my bright light either.

I wanted to explore, travel the world and live overseas. When would I be able to do that?

I realised I struggled with my beliefs, too, which were contradictory to what I wanted to do. As much as I criticised society's expectations and beliefs regarding women and success, it seemed I had taken them on board, too!

I was having a fight with myself.

I wanted a successful career in medicine. But I believed a lot of hard work was needed to succeed and also that a successful career is tiring. With that in mind, I realised I habitually chose to do difficult things, aiming to feel tired.

I was bothered by the fact that I created obstacles for everything I did because I was a hero and a saviour, and a hero needs challenges to be heroic and save others.

I wanted good relationships, but I believed some people were jealous of me and out there to get me.

I wanted to create a coaching service for young people, but I believed I was not a good leader, so how could I do such a thing?

I wanted to write a book, but I believed no one would want to read a book by me.

I wanted wealth, but I believed a lot of money creates trouble, especially if you are a female with money; you can be fooled by people who want to be close to you to get money from you.

I wanted to live a happy life, but I did not want regrets.

I wanted to be independent, and I did not want anyone supporting me.

The list went on. Over the years that followed medical school, I worked on my beliefs and fears with the help of self-help books, because at that time that is all I could find in Sri Lanka. With that, I achieved some success in getting over myself. Life became happier; I was making progress.

Later, after I moved to Australia, I sought professional support from counsellors and coaches. Not just one or two – many. I was always working on myself, which also made me tired. I felt like I was pushing against something all the time. After all those years of work, I was still fighting with myself.

Was there a way not to push against yourself and just be happy?

How could I simplify my life so that I could do just one thing?

What is the one thing I could have that would grant me all my wishes and dreams?

I became qualified as a coach and it gave me unlimited access to many helpful people in the coaching industry. I was busy undoing my mess for a few years afterwards and I understood it didn't stop. Just as you discovered the root of a problem, you would see a spot that could be improved slightly more.

Despite all that, my life was painful.

People have always admired me for my perseverance in whatever I do. But that does not mean I have to do everything over long periods of time, jumping over many hurdles. You need perseverance when you need it; it does not have to be a lifestyle.

While it was painful, I still dreamed of a good life. I never turned my back on that dream. But the problem was there were many obstacles between me and that dream becoming a reality.

As I incorporated coaching into my work toolbox, I opened a path to achieving the life I was looking for. I felt like God finally heard my wishes and gave me the magic wand to create the magical life I was after.

If you wish your dreams to be a reality, you must act on them. Without actions, the dream is only a dream.

Have *you* ever had a dream that excited you so much it kept you awake at night and made you jump out of bed in the morning? Was that dream so big you were unsure where to start?

My dream for a life with no regrets was like that. I had suffered so much living without an aim, and my vision for this big exciting life was my saviour. It kept me going all the time, beyond any challenges I faced.

I dreamed of living a rich, luxurious life – a life without regrets.

Not only would my future be beautiful, but I also wanted to change how people lived for the better in a bigger way. How could I do that? I wondered. It felt like it was beyond my imagination and out of my reach. But from experience, I knew it would become attainable with relentless work. Despite feeling overwhelmed, I pushed through and understood how my brain responded to a dream that stretched my imagination.

I knew that because of how I operated when I wanted to achieve something. I realised that to achieve anything, I must first know myself and what I wanted clearly. My life circumstances were such that anything I had achieved so far in my life was unimaginable at some point when the idea began in my head for the first time.

However, I realised knowing myself meant understanding my brain's strengths and weaknesses and how it operated to help me survive.

Reflecting on my life, I realised I only had one dream my whole life. All the goals, dreams and plans were to do one thing.

I wanted to live my beautiful life – the life I came here to live.

I came here to live my life, not someone else's.

What do I mean by that?

My beautiful life would allow me to be unique and fully express myself without shrinking to fit in with others around me. Others would not dictate the life I came here to live. My life would evolve with me and keep me occupied, so I could continue creating it as long as I live, and have nothing to catch up on at any point. That kind of life would not stress me about the unfinished work but keep me overjoyed about my achievements. That life might feel lazy, but it would be extremely productive. I would have many loving connections and friends, yet still feel comfortable enough to give my introverted self the privacy she needs.

Then I realised there is something called a brain that I must work with. The brain helps us to escape danger, make decisions, survive, and maintain the body you occupy. Without a brain, there is no thinking or thought. Without a brain, there is no processing or understanding of happiness or sadness, fear or bravery, anger or compassion, grief or expectations, shame or dignity, guilt or innocence.

The brain helps us to live and maintain our physical body and the functions of the mind and connect with what is external to our physical existence. The physical environment is where other living beings and creations of nature meet and greet as we all evolve together, along with the evolution of the earth, the solar system, the universe, the atmosphere and all the bits and pieces yet to be invented.

The brain is connected to the five senses: sight, smell, hearing, taste and touch. Through the five senses, the brain receives information that then gets processed to be expressed with the help of the mind.

So, considering all of this, I ask: who am I?

I have a brain, a body and a mind. The body has arms and legs and all the other structures called organs. I cannot be my brain because I can't simultaneously be 'my brain' and me. I'm not my body because then I must be 'my body' and myself at the same time. I'm not my thoughts or the mind from where the thoughts originate because I realise I cannot have a mind and be the mind at the same time.

Who am I then?

I am a free spirit, a force of energy beyond my physical body and abstract attributes.

In medical school, I dissected human bodies to learn anatomy. The bodies of dead people were kindly donated for the medical students to study and learn from and use that knowledge to save humans from diseases.

Who died when the body died? The body indeed died, but what happened to whoever used that body? I was not given any instructions to find a 'mind' inside the dead body as I dissected it. It is common knowledge that a mind cannot be touched or felt with the five senses. A mind knows what the five senses provide as information, but no one knows how to locate it inside the body.

Amazing!

Everyone accepts that there is a mind, irrespective of their age or level of education. People understand the concept of having a mind, although they are not aware of where it is. Everyone knows the mind is intangible; it cannot be touched with the hands. The mind is not something humans invented, but something humans arrived with.

Certainly, no one has to know where to find it to use it. But does anyone know how to stop using it? People quit using the body when they kill themselves, ending life by suicide, but can a person kill a mind? If you had a choice to end your life as you wish, should you kill the body or the mind? If a person is not the mind or their body, what should you kill to escape your suffering if you must?

I would say you kill your existence if you must … because there is no point in killing a physical body when there is an existence that is not your intangible mind or the physical body.

How do you kill an existence if you must?

I don't know how to kill my existence, but I do know how to *improve* my existence – by changing how I perceive myself.

> *I'm sad for you, my friend, as killing yourself was what you chose for a reason unknown to all of us left behind. It doesn't look like suicide was a great idea, as it probably did not kill your existence, at least as far as I know. Why do people kill the physical body when the mind is hurting? Bad idea. There is medicine to cure hurting minds and hurting bodies these days. You don't have to kill them to cure it. To cure, you must go on.*
>
> *If you are sure you cannot be cured, you must stop your existence – but only if you know how.*
>
> *But how will you know without a body and a mind? We need the physical body and the abstract mind to live on Earth. You must physically exist to work out the way to end existence!*
>
> *Hmmm.*

How is this mind–body jargon even important in a book about a life without regrets? As far as I know, the mind and the body help create a life, and this book is about creating a life and respecting our existence.

If I'm achieving any goal in this human experience, I must use my brain, body and mind as my tools, knowing all their limitations in helping me. I aim to live a happy, easy, abundant life where I can fully express myself as a unique human. Talking about the brain and how it works, it is important to know that the brain processes information by using labels or categorising them to make associations with similar ones.

I realised the struggle I was having with myself around being an achiever and how that had a connection with the words I used to describe what I wanted.

I wanted to enter medical school, and I added specificity by describing my goal: I wanted to enter medical school in the faculty of Medicine at the University of Colombo. I achieved my goal. I realised the more specific and clear the goal was, the easier it was to achieve.

I wanted a happy, successful life with no regrets – but what does anyone understand by that? That goal could be interpreted in many ways depending on the person reading it. It had no specificity other than having no regrets.

When I identified my goal as 'a happy life', what I meant was a life without regrets. After all, I already had regrets, and I did not want more. All I wanted was an easy, abundant life where I could fully express myself and be unique. Abundance is how I would explain everything I wanted in one word now, but back then, I had never heard of that word, so I did not know how to use it to explain my goal. Even the words 'abundance' and 'fully expressing myself' could be interpreted in many ways. I began to think there was a problem with clarity in my goal.

I wanted to express my uniqueness; I realised that happens when others do not dictate to me.

I thought being a doctor would let loose the saviour in me.

I wanted a happy life; I thought a happy life meant having no regrets.

So, here was my new life goal: a life without regrets, and being a doctor not dictated to by others.

If you are reading this book, you are clearly interested in a life without regrets. To create such, first you must know what you mean by that and be able to put it into words clearly and specifically.

You also need to align your mind, body and spirit so that you can communicate effectively with all parts of yourself to achieve your life goal. The more you know how to better communicate with yourself – mind, body and spirit – the better you will be at easily achieving your goal.

Mind is an abstract concept used to explain human experiences and behaviour.

The brain and all the other organs that form the human body have limitations in terms of physical existence.

The spirit is unlimited abundance and a flow of energy.

Why do you need to communicate with your body in goal setting? Your body represents your physical existence. When you set a goal, you communicate with yourself holistically. The goal must be ecological for you and your circumstances. You use words to communicate with yourself, and the words you use influence what you do and how you do it.

Let me ask you a question. *How are you doing today?*

Most of us would commonly say, 'I'm okay, thank you.' Try saying it – at least quietly. Now, observe how you feel. Are you excited? Happy? Or are you just existing because you happen to be here? Now, answer my question by saying, 'Fantastic, life could not be better.' Say it aloud. Do you feel the difference? Your body may have felt a different energy level; your posture may have changed even slightly; and your face may have had a different expression. I'm guessing you had to smile as you said it. Right?

That is a simple example of how your words or use of linguistics can influence how you do things and how you physically respond to the words you use. You respond to different words differently. If you want to feel different and change your thinking and behaviour, you must use your language carefully to tailor the outcome.

Neuro-linguistic programming (NLP) is a tool that can help people communicate better. Professional life coaches use it to provide support to their clients. NLP helps people communicate effectively using linguistics and understand themselves better.

NLP is a process that explains what we do and why we do it using linguistics as a key to unlock the information that is not readily available to us at a conscious level. You do not need to be a coach to use it; it explains patterns of thinking and behaviour people already use and allows them to modify these patterns by becoming more aware of them.

NLP explains what we do when we use linguistics – it is not an invention. So, even if you know NLP or not, you use it already, but you may need an awareness of its power over you.

By nature, the human mind likes to follow directions. It constantly looks for what it likes. So, if you ask your mind to get you something you like, it will work on it day and night and get it to you the easiest way possible. The mind can work on anything while the body sleeps.

For example, have you ever experienced that something you like attracts your attention when you think of it? At one stage in my life, I thought of buying a Mercedes. I looked in the online catalogue and selected the ones I liked. Suddenly, I started noticing more and more Mercedes on the road when I drove. I would drive in one direction and suddenly be craning my neck to look at a Mercedes parked on the side of the road. Have you ever experienced anything like that? I wouldn't have noticed the Mercedes parked on the road without my attention being redirected to it. I did not actively look for it, but something else made my head turn that way so I would notice it. I have driven on the same roads for years without noticing any Mercedes. Once I became interested in Mercedes, I experienced roads full of Mercedes! That was my unconscious mind at work. It understood I liked Mercedes and showed me more and more of what I liked.

While a Mercedes might be something nice to notice, the same can also work for something not so nice – like regrets. Your brain understands what you like by how much you think about it. You think of Mercedes, it shows you Mercedes. If you think of regrets, it shows you regrets. I didn't want regrets, but by using those words and telling myself that repeatedly, I gave my brain the goal of creating regrets.

If you don't want something, don't think about it.

One fundamental characteristic of the mind is that it does not process negatives. In other words, it doesn't understand anything presented with 'not xyz'. It only understands 'xyz'. It also likes to make associations for the convenience of delivering a message.

If I tell myself, 'I don't like regrets,' my unconscious mind will process it as 'I like regrets.'

If you are like me and many other people, we commonly use the word 'not' to describe things we like. For example, a person may say, 'I don't want to be tired,' meaning they like feeling fresh.

So, I wanted a life without regrets and to be a doctor not dictated to by others. As I continued living my young life, I added a few other things to this goal.

I did not want to be poor. I liked hard work and believed success came with hard work. I believed doctors didn't need leadership skills; therefore, the title of doctor suited me because I did not have leadership skills. Do you see the limiting beliefs I was imposing on myself?

So this is the expanded version of the goal I created:

A life without regrets, being a doctor not dictated to by others, not living poorly, success through hard work, and believing I had poor leadership skills.

What my brain truly understood out of that description is:

A life of regrets, a doctor dictated by others, success through hard work, living poorly and believing I had poor leadership skills.

At one stage of my life, I had achieved that goal precisely. I did come to see I was responsible for my mess – but only when my life had become unbearable. At that point, I needed to reflect on my actions and experiences to understand what was happening to me.

When I understood how my brain and mind work, I was not surprised how my goals had manifested so perfectly. Until I switched my thinking to describe what I wanted to be *exactly* what I wanted, I was a slave to other people's opinions of me and a hard-working achiever who believed they had no leadership skills. I earned money; I always had money, but I behaved as if I was poor. I was always worried about money. I felt I did not have enough money. I was scared to spend money or to buy anything for myself. I was in debt because I saw debt as a way of acquiring wealth. I was not paying attention to my finances – in fact, I avoided looking at my bank account, as I was too scared to see it empty. Ironically, I always had more than enough in my bank account – even in my most desperate moments. The more effort I made to earn money, the poorer I felt. In order to be successful and rich, I was working even harder. The more effort I made to be happy, the sadder I felt. I wondered what had happened to the bubbly youngster I once was. I regretted my decisions, how I acted and many more things about my life.

For me, happiness was about getting rid of sadness. I was looking for happiness, but my true goal was sadness. I realised I was sad by default. I only saw sadness in life. Life was precisely the opposite of what I wanted because I set a goal of exactly the opposite of what I wanted by aiming for a life without the things I did not like.

Do you understand what I'm telling you? My brain has helped me to have everything I wanted, and it's not the brain that went wrong; it was me. I just had to change how I used words to create goals so my brain understood what I wanted.

The human mind has been studied through evolving science,

and its functions have been explained through various theories; psychology experts may know them in much better detail than I do.

If you would like to achieve a goal, you must precisely describe what you would like to have for you to have it. If you cannot describe something in words, you cannot have it, which means you do not know what you want. So, if you don't describe and put a name to something, it does not exist in your reality. You only see what you already know. As in the example of the red rose I described in the previous chapter, you don't know what you don't know. You only know what you know.

When I was growing up, I never knew the word 'abundance' or phrases such as 'fully expressing myself'. They were not part of the culture I grew up in. I could not even comprehend these terms or their meanings because I'd never heard them, so I could not use them directly until I learned more about them. I could only explain what I knew of my goal using the words I knew and understood!

Living a beautiful and exciting life is different from living without regrets. You could live without regrets and not have an exciting and beautiful life.

When you live without regrets, you run away from a life of regrets, i.e. a life you don't want to live. You move towards your desired life when you live a beautiful and exciting life. They are not the same.

If you want to achieve your goals, you need a goal to move towards, not one to run away from. You can never finish running away from something undesirable; you will continue running away as long as you are focused on outrunning the fear. But you can move in a different desired direction if you have that as your goal.

But you need to know what you *want*, not what you *don't* want.

Being rich is not the same as escaping poverty. Because you can be neither rich nor poor, but somewhere in between. Or you could be rich but still feel and act poor.

Being healthy is not the same as not being unhealthy. Healthy is an optimally balanced state of physical and emotional well-being. You can be not unhealthy, but not in optimal well-being either.

Happy is the opposite word to unhappy, but finding happiness and getting rid of unhappiness are two different things. You can be neither happy nor unhappy, but somewhere in between.

When you run away from an unwanted situation, you enter what's known as 'survival mode'. This mode is how your body operates to escape danger. It's a pre-prepared set of events or procedures that your brain activates to ensure your safety. Think of it as a fire alarm: when the alarm sounds, people evacuate the building, the fire truck arrives and the fire is extinguished. Similarly, when you perceive you are being threatened, your body enters 'fight or flight' mode, which minimises some bodily functions and modifies energy expenditure to prepare your body to move faster and escape. Your pupils dilate so you can see; your heart beats faster and pumps more blood to the muscles you need to move; you breathe faster to get more oxygen into your lungs, and blood circulation to your brain and essential organs increases to help you operate more effectively. Functions such as digestion and sexual function slow down, as they are not necessary for the fight-or-flight response.

In summary, when you are in survival mode, your body is ready to fight or flee but is not ready for pleasurable activities. This is also known as the stress response. The longer you remain in this state, you become chronically stressed as your body's stress response becomes your default mode. The slightest trigger can provoke you; you are hyper-alert, looking for danger to stay safe as you run away from what you fear.

I realised I had been living in survival mode by default, running away from what I feared. Fear of being poor and being dictated to by others. I wanted to take control of my life to ensure I was not dependent on someone else's poor planning to ensure I was living well. I did not want to depend on others who could not provide for themselves. Being independent was good, but I refused to let others support me out of love and kindness. I was refusing to receive, merely to prove I could support myself. I was looking for everything I was not particularly eager to have to ensure I was safe.

I realised I had spent a long time escaping life instead of living it. The danger I was trying to escape was within myself, and I couldn't outrun it. Instead, I had to face it and make changes within myself, not outside of me.

As I've already mentioned, when I was 19, I decided that goal setting was too tiring, and I wanted to take a break. I thought I would rejuvenate myself and start over, but I never did. Goal setting is painful when you only focus on what you need to achieve in one aspect of life.

It was not unreasonable to expect to succeed in my studies because, in my circumstances, that was a guaranteed way of surviving the harshness of the economy. A doctor was guaranteed success in the job market. There was a war up north in Sri Lanka and civil riots and disturbances down south; we were squashed between two groups of terrorists clashing with the government and public, disturbing everyone's lives. Death by violence was common. Suicide bombers were everywhere; the country was in survival mode. No one knew if they would be alive the next day for many long years.

I used to condition myself for success using visualisations regularly – and I realised it worked when I got into medical school. Conditioning myself for success gave me reassurance that there was a way to end suffering by becoming a doctor. It worked as a self-affirmation that helped me remain committed and motivated.

After achieving my victorious milestone in entering medical school, I wanted to relax and not be so stressed – so I thought stopping goal setting would help me achieve that instead of addressing the stress. Some agreed with me; I've heard others say that goal setting makes them stay alert and too focused and ignore other things they want. It was natural to feel tired living in a country ridden by war over decades. What I could have rejuvenated – if I knew how – was my thoughts.

Four years after my decision to not set any goals, I found myself with no direction in life, feeling like a failure, being bullied and crying almost every day because I was living with no aim in mind. When you don't give a direction of your own in life, life will take you in the direction others decide for you. That is a guaranteed way of losing control over your life. My idea at that time was to stop goal setting to rejuvenate myself, and now I understand why it did not work.

But can you ever escape goal setting in life?

What I needed to understand at that young age is that one can never escape goal setting because, in the human mind, goal setting happens by default. One characteristic of the mind is that it sets one goal after another; the only thing you can do about it is to give your mind a useful goal.

Whether you decide to set goals or not, you have given your mind a goal.

When you decide on a goal, you have instructed your mind on the direction you want to take in your life.

When you decide not to set goals, you direct your mind not to set goals and live life without goals. Either way, you have given a direction and set a goal.

By setting a goal, you direct your life as you want. When you don't set a goal, you direct your life to live without a direction. In the latter case, life gives you direction, and you float wherever everyday events and experiences take you.

In the latter situation, you no longer have control of your life, because you have let others control your life. If you want to control that situation, you must take control over what you think and do, and be responsible for your own life and decisions.

It took me four years of directionless pain to understand I needed to change things. It took many years thereafter to completely change the situation and take control of my life back into my own hands again, but that is not the be-all and end-all.

You could be in control of one aspect of life, but not another. You may be powerless in some ventures in your life, but not in others. It is an ongoing process to ensure that you function responsibly in each of the different categories of life, as life categories change and update as you grow older. You discover more aspects of you that need work done as you mature.

Letting others direct how you live and not taking responsibility for yourself is called living 'at effect' – or letting things happen to you. When you live at effect, you make excuses and blame others for the life you live. You have no control over life and let others decide what you do for you. You feel powerless, and life becomes unpredictable as external factors decide how you live it.

The opposite of living at effect is called living 'at cause'. It is a powerful position to place yourself in if you want to make any changes in your life. When you live at cause, you take one hundred per cent responsibility for yourself; therefore, you can change your experiences. Instead of blaming others, you look within yourself to see where and what could change. You are in total control of your life.

It is important to note that a person can be in a mixture of living at effect and living at cause in different aspects of their life.

I ran away from regretting rather than forgiving myself for not taking control of my life.

There was a drastic difference between the daredevil who entered medical school and the heartbroken young doctor who left it.

The daredevil was known for her spine of steel, her no-fear attitude and the kindness that flowed through her veins. She believed in herself, found ways to do the impossible and was self-satisfied and happy by default; no one bothered her and no one challenged her.

The heartbroken young woman had lost control of her life and her superpowers, focus and self-trust. She operated from fear, lack and limiting beliefs and, in a state of suffering, had to push herself to keep her dreams alive.

Instead of growing into the person her future warranted, the heartbroken young doctor hid away with a fear of failure, ridden with limiting beliefs such as her not having what it took to be a good leader. She believed success came with hard work, so she did everything the difficult way because, according to her theory, the more successful you are, the harder your life will be.

I was too busy ensuring I was successful and hiding from what my future might offer. Surely, for example, there could have been more fun. But if I had fun, I would not succeed! I had a clear demarcation between living and working/studying. For me, studying/working was the main reason to live, and having fun and not pursuing goals became the mode I used to refuel myself.

I realised that lifestyle was a problem, though. At a very fundamental level, people work to earn money to live. What's the purpose of working and earning if you don't spend that money to live? The work has to support and uplift living. Work allows you to live better – you don't have to live to work.

I spent countless hours wondering how to be the daredevil again. I spent hours with coaches and counsellors to work out what to do, with no luck. But with all that inner work, I was untangling my messy head and getting rid of those limiting beliefs I had grown over the years. The longer you stay with limiting beliefs, the messier your thoughts will be, as mess attracts more mess, leading to more and more mess.

The daredevil believed what she wanted was good, and she could achieve it. The heartbroken youngster had a lot of contradictory beliefs about what she wanted to do:

- I'm not a good leader.
- Money is bad.
- People are evil.
- A successful life is tiring.

There were more; these are a few examples.

When you work towards your goal, you need a belief system that helps you achieve what you want. If your beliefs do not align with your goal, you create an inner resistance that slows you down. Your goal has to be something you fully agree with in terms of your values and beliefs. If not, you need to re-visit your goal to see if you really want it or change your belief system so that you do not create an inner fight with your actions.

That belief could be yours, or you may have borrowed it from somebody else, depending on your circumstances. When I grew up, I borrowed a lot of beliefs from people around me and came to some life-changing decisions based on them. For example, I saw success as tiring. That's because I'd seen how tirelessly people work to achieve success and how messy their personal lives can be. So, to me, success meant having a tiring professional life and a messy personal life. As I went on, I created that and found work was getting harder, and life, messier. I found my goals moving away from me and taking a long time to manifest, because I did not want them on a certain level.

That mess cleared over the years when I worked on it, but the biggest jump came the day I decided to act on the goals I had always wanted and to stop running away from fears. It gave my life a purpose. When I was clear on my life purpose, I was clear on what beliefs I needed to be that person who lived her life's purpose.

When you live your purpose and grow into what you need to be, your life and work become one. There is nothing to balance in such a life.

You need to understand work–life balance to create a life that is rejuvenating in itself, so that you don't need to stop and run away from goal setting like I did.

Many of us tend to balance work and life. But I'm here to tell you that the concept of work–life balance is a myth. What is real is goal setting that is ecological and authentic to the person and the context. The reality is that if you are living, you have a goal: whether the goal is specific or termed as having 'no goals', either way you work on your goals as you live. Living is a process of goal achieving. That is why you cannot separate living from working. All you can do is aim for the process of goal achieving to become pleasurable, so you can continue on without having to stop and rejuvenate.

Life is a process of goal achievement. You are born destined to die; you move from the point of birth to the point of death. In-between, you do many things that are labelled 'living life'. Some things get labelled as 'work', and others get labelled as 'living'. Using two labels to describe what you do as you live creates a separation between the two. When you separate what you do into two categories, you are doomed to keep maintaining a balance between the two.

When you have separated work from living, you create a need to stop and rejuvenate. If you are looking to stop and rejuvenate, you are running away and looking to re-stock the energy you lost in running. Life is not comparable to a motor vehicle where the tank needs to be filled to supply energy for the journey.

If you are living the process your goal requires you to live, your energy will be used effectively, and there will be no need to stop to conserve it. You will not lose energy as you live, but convert energy to different forms. For example, the energy you consume in your food gets converted to the muscles that move you, the thoughts that you think and the services you exchange with others. Living is a way of exchanging energy. If you exchange your energy effectively, you do not need to rejuvenate to fill the tank again.

You do not have to stop having fun to be a doctor. Instead, you could learn how to have fun and still be a doctor. You could be what your end goal demands of you: for example, your goal might be to be a doctor *and* have holistic growth in mind, body and soul. If you can have the mental and emotional qualities a doctor needs and be in the optimum physical state to be energetic and healthy, and if you have a system in place to ensure these get upgraded as you go, you are living the goal of being a doctor and enjoying it. Is there a reason to stop that process to 'rejuvenate'?

You are living life and doing work that makes you feel like you are living a fulfilled life.

Otherwise, stopping to rejuvenate and address work–life balance will never end because work and life changes and evolves as we live, and the need for balance arises with the labels we put on them. What would you call it if your work was also your hobby?

What if I tell you that anyone can have a life so fulfilling that work becomes life and life becomes work?

What label would you give to your work if you converted your work into a rejuvenating experience?

What if your work became something you loved to do and let you have fun and grow as a human while creating wealth?

I have experienced both – a life stuck in the work–life balance myth, and a life doing the work I absolutely love doing.

Does the latter give me money to live? Yes, it does, and I'm actually better off than ever before.

The day I declared I was no longer doing the work–life balance myth, I started seeing my life as a continuous process of achieving what I wanted ecologically. I realised for that process to be ecological, there must be self-fulfilment with whatever I do. I realised I feel more fulfilled when I am doing what my soul likes.

Previously, I was always focused on work; I had no time for what made me feel fulfilled, as work only represented some of the things I liked doing on a regular basis. I liked my work, but there was this constant feeling of lack or missing out. I was seeking work–life balance to eliminate the feeling of missing out, when what I should have been doing was to stop seeing work as work and life as life. Instead of achieving work–life balance, I decided to create the ideal life that would give me a feeling of fulfillment in and of itself. So, I began doing what my soul had been whispering in my ears for many years: writing a book, public speaking, serving people internationally, coaching people, being wealthy beyond limits, and spending time with family and friends.

My work calendar now has all those elements incorporated in it. Work has become life and life has become work – there are no longer two separate labels. If I were to put one label on that calendar, it would be 'things I like'.

And there is no need to label things I don't like – what matters is defining those I do.

The day I decided to do that, I started living my big life – being myself.

With that, I made a quantum leap in my life that changed my story from that of a people-pleaser and hard-working achiever to a self-dictated, happy person. It did not take me years to accomplish the things my soul had been whispering in my ear; simply deciding with certainty what I was going to do and taking initial steps towards those goals made my soul settle, and suddenly, my life became completely different; there was a calmness and focus to my days that I hadn't experienced before.

I could be myself anywhere now I was simply just living my life. I had only one version of myself; there was no need to adjust myself for certain work situations or life circumstances. Instead, I was genuine everywhere I went and in whatever I did.

As I allowed myself to dictate what I did and fully express my uniqueness, my life became simpler. My life was my work. When I worked, I created life.

When I focused on the bigger, simpler life, I started growing into someone who could meet the challenges of a big life. Life became only a matter of growth. Growing into the person I needed to be was fun; there was no need for harmful self-criticism. You just had to grow and know where you needed to go. I continued to grow; there was no need to stop what I did to rejuvenate. I self-rejuvenate as I go.

I'm finally at home.

I'm not talking about you physically exerting yourself all day – physical existence has its limits. The mind does not. I'm not talking about engaging in tasks that need a higher level of focus all the time. The length of your attention span changes with age and the tasks you do. What I'm saying is the moment you give something a label, your brain requires a comparison, as that is how it identifies things. You need to be careful of the labels you give and the words you use.

When you label something 'work', there are things that are automatically labelled 'not work'. You can live while you work and not work. Living is a bigger frame that encompasses working and not working.

When you label what you do as 'living', another label can arise as 'not living'. You cannot live and not live at the same time. Because when you do not live, you are dead. You cannot be living and dead at the same time. If there is any other label to encompass both living and dead, it would be existing.

When you see everything you do as living, you get to see the bigger picture. The bigger picture makes life simple. It lets you organise and categorise to make sense.

When you see work as separate from living, you are stuck in a little corner, unable to grasp the whole picture or the life you create. That creates the mental exhaustion many of us experience out of overwhelm by not knowing where we are going with our lives and a feeling of being unfulfilled.

Work–life balance cannot be achieved by equal distribution of time among tasks or allocating time for 'work' and 'life' regularly. It cannot be achieved by alternating periods of time where you work or rejuvenate. You cannot achieve something that does not exist; you cannot achieve it because it is a myth.

What exists is life. Work is a concept created by a label used to describe certain things you do.

Work generally represents something you like to do. It is unlikely that you would be doing a job if it involved a type of work you completely disagreed with. At least something must attract you to that type of work. It is your job to ensure you do what you like to do as you live. You are more fulfilled in life when you do what you like.

Seeing the big picture of your life lets you simplify the different things you do. Imagine getting to a mountaintop to see what's around you. Climbing a mountain is tiring. What would happen if you got into a helicopter and rose up above the mountain? You would see the mountaintop and the other things that surround the mountain.

When you see the big picture of your life, it is easy for you to work out the details of it. I did that when I removed the work–life balance myth from my head.

When you think in terms of work–life balance and create work that needs to be balanced with life, you are like a mountain climber. Climbing a mountain, no matter how big or small, is tiring. Even if you climb to the top, there may be another mountain you need to climb for you to see the surroundings clearly. That is non-stop mountain climbing; you would definitely feel the need to give up at some point because there is no end in sight. That's not the right way to see your surroundings.

In trying to achieve work–life balance, I had no time for many of the things I wanted to do.

When I stopped trying to achieve this balance and started doing everything I *liked* instead, I had time to do everything I wanted and more. People always have time for the things they really like to do. It's just a matter of what you like to do most.

You might think that I would struggle with my time, doing many more things. But no, I have a lot of time now – because I am only doing one thing. That one thing is called living my life. Living my life is how I spend my time. That is simple, sure – but it's big enough to keep me interested and curious about how I unfold myself as I grow.

With that in mind, I gradually started doing things my way. It was slow but steady. I did things deliberately to ensure they happened just the way I wanted. I had a bad habit of pleasing everyone; now, I was pleasing only one person – me.

I started to write this book three years before it was published, but it did not progress because I was too scared to put my name on it. *Who wants to read a book written by Lakshinie Gunasiri? Even the name was a bad choice!*

I started writing this book and put my name on the first page. Done.

I gave myself small daily opportunities to do what I liked, the way I liked. I planted roses in the backyard, knowing a rose-eating possum was killing my plants! *How dare you! Do you know I own this land, and you are an animal without boundaries?*

When no humans are around to bully you, sometimes even a plant-eating animal can bully you. I fought with the possum for years, trying to grow what I liked. I gave up in the end and started being 'sensible' – which meant buying plants the possum would not want to eat. But I soon lost interest in the garden because there were no plants in it that I liked. Then, I decided I'd had enough of being dictated to by a possum. I grew what I liked and felt a new level of motivation entering my veins. The possum ate them, but I didn't care anymore. What mattered was my enjoyment of the garden. After all, I couldn't stop the possum admiring my garden! The land was mine, but the possum didn't know that. If I showed my deed of ownership to the possum, would it be able to read English and understand what it said? To me, this tiny bit of land is mine; to the possum, the whole area is its territory. I'm not sure who the real landlord is.

I decorated my home just the way I would like it to be. I started mentally preparing for public speaking by coming out of my shell. I allocated coaching to my calendar. I started organising my day, so it was easier to do what I did than do things to fit others' needs.

The more I did things my way, the easier life became. Life was about me again after a long time. I became happier and calmer. I had more time. I had more clarity in my head, and whatever I did became more efficient, giving me more time to do the things I liked. Time became a fascinating playground for me to play the game of life. My life started feeling cosy, like a holiday, and the holiday craving I had disappeared. My weekends and holidays became an experience I enjoyed rather than an escape from what I did not enjoy.

All I did was stop running away from what I did not like and move towards what I liked instead – those are the things I loved to do – as opposed to doing what others thought I should do.

Whatever I did was whatever I deeply desired to do. I realised the more I fought with myself, the more detours I created for myself, and my goals took longer to achieve. Whenever I did something along the lines of my deepest desires, they were quick to manifest in the external world. Those desires were the ones I decided on my own without anyone else's opinion or permission.

Basically, I stopped fighting myself.

As I started doing things I had always dreamed of, I became more confident in myself and my abilities.

When I did what I always wanted, simply because I liked doing it, I found my life's purpose. I realised that my purpose on this earth was to live my life to the fullest. As I lived my life, I served the world. I did not serve to live anymore, instead I let my living become a service to others. That way, there was only one person to deal with. Me.

There is no confusion about priorities or questions about how to have everything without sacrificing one thing for another. What others think does not matter anymore; what matters is how much I enjoy watching *me* grow. There are no failures or successes. I decide how I label what I do. When there is no failure, there is no fear of failure; I only need to be accountable for myself.

I do what I enjoy, and money follows. In the past, I had to do what I knew to earn a living. Now, I don't earn money, but rather, I embody it. Money comes as I live doing what I like to do. I'm money. I'm at home.

Give your life direction

YOUR LIFE WORK

1. Reflect on your life and identify if you run away from certain things. Write them down.

2. Next, create a goal under each topic you have listed that you could move towards. Example: run away from poverty – the goal: create wealth.

3. Check with yourself how you feel about the goal you wrote. Do you truly desire the goal?

4. What do you believe in relation to that goal?

5. If anything is possible, and if you had all the money and resources you needed, what service would you be offering to the rest of the world in exchange for money?

6. How would you create the service you mentioned in number 5 if you were the only person in the world who could offer such a service?

    - What would you add to your service that no one else could offer?

    - What would you not have in your service compared to what your peers would offer?

3

Trust yourself

*Cultivate an attitude of self-trust,
forgiveness, and gratitude.*

If you lack self-trust, it reflects in your actions and behaviour, making others lose trust in you. This lack of trust can lead to a lack of commitment and failure. When you're in doubt, asking for advice can be helpful, but remember that people advise you based on their perspective, not necessarily yours. Following other people's advice may lead you to something similar to but different from what you want. You need your vision and trust in yourself to create the life you want. This trust is especially crucial when things don't go as planned. It helps you hold yourself accountable and ultimately builds more self-trust. After all, why would others trust you if you don't trust yourself?

I vividly remember the day I made three life-altering decisions and set goals around them: to start a life coaching service, write a book and specialise in medicine.

It was a beautiful sunlit morning in April 2001. I was walking across an open area in the medical school when an idea came into my head, followed by another, followed by another. That was it. The first was to establish a coaching service for university students like me, and the next was to write a book about how to move on with life and not cry when things don't go your way. I was already headed towards my third goal of specialising in medicine since I was at medical school.

It was a time of transition – between being a student and stepping into practice as an intern in medicine. But since that day, I have not turned back from those decisions. I didn't discuss it with anyone – there was no need for anyone's approval. I was going to do it. Once I'd made these decisions, I didn't feel pressured; instead, it gave me direction. Those three decisions were a key part of the life I was creating – the one without regrets.

A lot has happened since then, but that does not matter. What matters is what I did about these goals and how I went about it.

April always signifies new beginnings for me; many significant events have happened in April in my life. April is a time of celebration in Sri Lanka, especially in the context of culture and traditions, where life was created around a cycle of hard work in the paddy field, harvesting crops and celebrating success. Sinhalese and Tamil people in Sri Lanka celebrate the new year in April. These celebrations and traditions are formed around resolving conflicts, forgiving and reconnecting; and from the perspective of the mindset coach I went on to become, identifying the patterns and systems that run our lives. Homes are whitewashed and cleaned, people dress up and prepare a feast together, enough to feed an entire village. People help each other, reconnect and exchange support, while taking time to have fun in a relaxed and forgiving atmosphere.

People are invited to visit each other's houses, form new connections while strengthening the old, and celebrate success with gratitude for those who have supported them thus far. The intention is also to move forward into the new year revamped with new energy.

I don't recall why I was there that day, in April 2001, when I made those decisions, but I knew where I was heading. I was moving towards a bigger future. I made those decisions, set those goals, and trusted the details would be known later.

If I summarise what I learned at medical school, apart from the medical training, I learned to overcome challenges and turn them into a blessing. My blessing out of medical school was my decision to have a career encompassing a non-medical aspect – to incorporate personal development into my career and the service I would offer. I now see this as a way of moving forward and wiping away all those tears. Reflecting back, it shows me the reasons for the difficulties I faced, as I had no strategies for resolving conflict at that point. Learning to forgive came years later.

Many things happened in my life as if out of a fairy tale – I met my husband-to-be; we got married; I was offered a great position in a renowned hospital in Australia; and we moved to a new country. It was challenging, restarting my medical career while settling into this new life and dealing with culture shock at the same time as losing my connections with all that was dear and familiar. Transitions were never my strength, and having to deal with this many was hard.

These experiences forced me to rediscover myself, my strengths and my weaknesses, and grow as a person beyond what I ever imagined. There were many times when it would have been easier to redirect my career down a different path, but I held on to my goals and readjusted myself to a new role, which has only brought me benefits. I did not give up because I wanted to be accountable for myself. I trusted in my ability to achieve my goals because what I wished for in my world became my reality. I've always achieved what I wished for. I have done it repeatedly, which gives me the confidence to say this and write it in a book I intend many people to read and learn from.

My long-term goals for a bigger future, outside my medical career, helped me to think outside the box and learn new ways of being productive, and I am grateful for the skills they have given me.

That is where forgiveness and gratitude come in. Integrating forgiveness and gratitude into my daily life allowed me to have more fun, save time and energy, and move forward faster. It also made me happier and more productive. The biggest problem I faced was not knowing how to forgive people. I wasn't sure what I needed to do – did I have to forgive someone and then behave as if nothing had happened? I couldn't understand. It was only when I did my training as a coach that I finally grasped the true meaning of forgiveness. Then when I started incorporating it into my daily routine, that's when I realised what a superpower being able to forgive is.

I have incorporated it as a daily practice for over three years now, and it has affected me immensely. The biggest shift it created was that I have moved from being an angry critic to an empathic observer. That alone saved me massive amounts of time and energy every day.

Let me explain by telling you a story. One day, I was working on my laptop, having a nice day, in the flow of what I was doing, when suddenly, I had a thought in my head about something my husband did. I felt instantly irritated. I can't even remember what it was – something very minor – I think it was about where he keeps his shoes after taking them off at the doorstep. I remember a flicker of anger in my head, and that was the last thing I remember from that day. Two days later, I was still trying to get back into the flow of things, where I had left my task half done. I had lost two days in anger, which was compounded when I realised how much time I was wasting trying to get over it. That is the power of anger and resentment. You can lose prolonged periods, if not a lifetime, in anger and resentment, making the most unresourceful choices and landing in destinations where you never thought you would end up. If you were to visit a jail, I'm sure you would see many stories where anger and resentment diverted lives. The jail does not have to be a physical one; you could spend years in a jail that you create for yourself within your mind. You then become a prisoner of your mind.

During those two days I had lost because of an angry thought, Earth continued to move in its orbit and completed two full rotations. While the rest of the world experienced two sunrises and two sunsets, I missed them because of my preoccupation with negative thoughts. I was in a world of anger and frustration and did not know how to calm myself down. I knew time was ticking, and that made me angrier. I experienced more and more anger, one angry thought attracting another. The original thought that ignited the anger in my head was not even anything worth mentioning; if I were to mark it on a scale of zero to ten, it would be way less than zero. But that's the power of anger to distract a person, affecting whatever they do. It showed me a faulty system I had in place for dealing with anger.

I knew I had to release this anger, but I did not know how until I realised that forgiveness is the gateway to releasing anger. I began to do a daily meditation to incorporate forgiveness, gratitude and compassion into my life, and it changed my life as I learned that I had to forgive myself before I forgive anyone else. A free version of my forgiveness meditation is available online at **www.prowesscoaching.com.au**.

I used to believe that when someone did something wrong, the universe would return the aftermath of their actions to them. After all, what you give is what you get. So I would let the universe handle things for me. I believed it would give people what they deserved for their so-called wrongful deeds. That was my way of resolving conflict. No wonder I had not-so-nice things happen in my life; after all, what you get is what you give. You wish badly for another, bad things happen to you. Your unconscious mind does not differentiate between you and others.

Just because someone else did something bad, why would you wish badly upon them and end up on the receiving end of your evil wishes for others? Only a person feeling very powerless would do that – and I used to be one.

The underlying emotion beneath anger, sadness, guilt, shame and grief is fear. Fear and other negative emotions are tools of the primitive brain that protect us from danger. Those negative emotions serve a purpose in ensuring our survival, although the significance has changed. Back in the days when humans lived in caves and hunted for food, those negative emotions protected us from approaching danger. These days, not everyone meets a roaring tiger first thing in the morning – unless the tiger comes from within your head in the form of a fearful thought. There is no need to run if the tiger is within your head; you just need to understand that the tiger can be tamed by thinking differently.

We still have the same primitive brain, but live under different circumstances. Anger is part of our protective mechanism against threatening events; what is not good is having that protection overrun all your systems until no system can function because of the fear of losing our protection.

Practising forgiveness allowed me to release anger. The more I did it, the more relieved I felt, and the more I understood how much anger I had against myself. Soon, I started forgiving myself for the mistakes I had made, missed opportunities, misunderstanding people, and not being perfect in all things.

The more forgiveness I had for myself, the less problematic my addiction to perfectionism became.

The more I forgave myself, the easier it was to forgive others. The more I forgave others, the less of a hostage I became in my mind. The more I forgave, the less I lived in my head entangled in thoughts. The more I forgave myself and others, the more effective I became, and I found more and more time for the things I needed to do.

Think of your home. As you live there every day, you accumulate dust and clutter, right? Unless you have a system to clean up your house, you will live amongst piles of unwanted clutter. You may clean up your house daily or weekly, or you may even ask someone to do it for you, and that is your system for a tidy and clean house. In the same way, regularly practising forgiveness is how you ensure your mind does not get clogged up with mental clutter and dust. A clear mind creates a clear life vision and helps you focus with the least distractions.

How regularly does one have to practise forgiveness? Daily.

I incorporate it daily into my morning meditation, which takes about twenty minutes. I forgive myself and others for anything from a big life event to minor things, such as raising my voice at my child. It helps me move forward rather than staying hooked on what happened yesterday.

When you forgive, you remove the negativity in your mind due to whatever the incident was. Forgiveness does not mean you meet your greatest enemy at his house for a hug or invite them to dinner at your place. You could always do that later if you wish, but that's not my point.

Like every other action, a thought precedes forgiveness – so firstly, you forgive the person in your mind. When you attempt to forgive someone, you try to understand what led them to do what they did and see it from their point of view. If you have a fresh look at what they did from a judgement-free perspective, you understand that we have different interpretations of what we experience. It makes it easy to understand that they may have had good intentions. The more you forgive, the more you see the actual intention.

Some people commit crimes to protect someone they love. Some people do things that are less than ideal to protect themselves. People get involved in a war to protect their country. Innocent young people get recruited to the armed forces to kill the enemy to protect the rest of the population from the invaders. There is often a good intention behind a person's actions, but it may not be so apparent in the heat of the moment as not everyone shares the same interpretation of the world around them.

We are constantly surrounded by beings with whom we interact. Humans and other living animals breathe in oxygen and exhale carbon dioxide, while trees use carbon dioxide for photosynthesis and growth. Humans and animals rely on plants and trees for various purposes, including food for survival. We interact with our environment continuously, even if we're unaware of it. We are never truly alone; even during moments of loneliness, we are part of a constant flow of energy and interaction with others and our surroundings.

We are always giving and receiving from other living beings and our environment. We give away mental and physical energy through our professional services, for which we receive payment in the form of money. We then use the money to buy food that provides us the energy to live and move our bodies, which may benefit others through our actions. This cycle is in motion day and night.

Our actions can be broadly categorised in the following ways:

1. Not good for you, not good for others, not good for the greater good.

An example of that would be an addiction to drugs. It does not do any good for you or others; instead, it creates problems for everyone.

2. **Good for you, not good for others, not good for the greater good.**

   An example of this would be to steal money to buy food. Buying food helps you survive, but what you did was a threat to everyone around you and yourself in the end.

3. **Good for you, good for others, not good for the greater good.**

   An example of this would be to create a business that is not environmentally friendly. It is good for you; the business gives you money, and you let others contribute by providing employment. But in the end, it is not good for the greater good or yourself.

4. **Good for you, good for others, good for the greater good.**

   An example of this would be creating a charity for the homeless. You serve yourself and your desire to help others, provide other people ways to contribute to this good deed, and improve and uplift the living standards of society.

As you can see, you cannot do anything good or bad for the greater good without affecting yourself because you are part of that greater good.

Life is always about you and others. When you receive, you allow others to give. Every thought, action and experience starts with you, even if it's meant for others. You receive something, at least a certain feeling, when you give. You do things for others because it lets you receive something. Preparing yourself to receive things that are good for you, others and the greater good is crucial. When you're ready to receive in this way, you let others give what's good for you and the greater good. You need to allow yourself to receive to maintain the giving–receiving cycle. Otherwise, you are depriving yourself and causing self-destruction – just like I was, feeling too independent and not wanting to receive support and love. When you are not prepared to receive, you are not giving sustainably. When you give without receiving, you feel a need to rejuvenate and refuel because you let your tank run dry, which is self-destructive. When you do what's disruptive to your existence, it affects others who interact with you, too.

In some situations, you must put yourself first, even if it appears selfish. For example, in an aeroplane crash, you must put your oxygen mask on first before helping others, including your child. You need to help yourself first to help others. Putting yourself first is essential in creating a beautiful and exciting life. But you must be clear about why you want a beautiful and exciting life. Is it good for you, others and the greater good? Your life may only feel good for you initially, but it can continually evolve to be good for others and the greater good in the future.

So now you understand you must put yourself first, and it is the same for other people, too. It may at first appear like their actions are only good for themselves, but when you understand their intention from their perspective, it is easy to forgive and forget.

Understanding your constant interaction with others throughout your life allows you to feel grateful for what you take for granted. There is a famous saying that everything essential in life is free. We do not pay for the fresh air or the sunlight that drives life on Earth. Rain supplies the water we need, and food is grown through the natural environment. If you have nothing to be grateful for, at least be grateful for the fresh air you breathe or your body that breathes without conscious command. If breathing was under our conscious control, would anyone be alive still?

The biggest benefit I received from practising gratitude daily is that I realised my strengths and weaknesses, and that I'm another imperfect human. I could accept myself for all my good *and* bad. The more grateful I was for myself, the easier I could forgive myself. Practising gratitude daily allowed me to appreciate others for what they do for me, sometimes even without my request. I felt a newfound gratitude for my husband for his companionship in life, and I felt grateful for my children for the happiness they brought me. It became much easier for me to understand other people's points of view. The more I appreciated them for who they were, the better connections I made.

Gratitude can be practised in many ways. Gratitude can be shown with a smile, a well-meaning word, a gentle hand touch or a loving gaze. It can be conveyed in an act of reciprocated kindness. Gratitude is an everyday practice. To ensure you incorporate it more regularly, I recommend incorporating it into something you do daily. It could be the journalling you do before bed. When you write down who you are grateful for and why you are grateful for them, you create new neural pathways in your brain that allow similar thoughts and actions. I practice gratitude during my morning meditation. That was a life changer for me.

Being grateful for myself for who I am and who I was in the past, and reflecting on what I did when I did what I had to do at various stages of my life, helped me forgive myself for many things I held myself accountable for. With forgiveness, I saw my failures as experiences that taught me valuable lessons. The more I forgave myself, the more I could forgive others. The more I forgave myself, the better my relationships became, because I could forgive others for what they did.

Like everything else, forgiveness starts with you. You need to learn to forgive yourself before you can learn to forgive others. How can you forgive someone else if you cannot even forgive yourself? You cannot give something you don't know. You cannot give something you don't have.

Forgiveness allowed me to move on without crying when things did not go as planned.

Forgiveness made it easy for me to be grateful, because I could see others for who they really were and how they contributed to my existence.

Gratitude and forgiveness go hand in hand; they let you connect with people at a deeper level and create a long-lasting bond. With regular practice of gratitude and forgiveness, I found the lack of connection disappearing from my life.

Then, I found the connection I was looking for.

I met her. The one I was always looking for.

People missed her bubbly laughter when she was not around.

Some could not take their eyes off her pretty face when she laughed until her eyes filled with tears and her cheeks turned crimson. Attractive with square shoulders and a tall slim figure, she did justice to any outfit, leaving a tinge of jealousy in the hearts of some. She was always discrete in her actions – the very reason why some found her a matter of curiosity. She was wise to see through any mess and find what she wanted. She was a daydreamer, known for secret smiles that would pop out in public as she immersed herself in her dreams day and night. Most of all, she was courageous enough to stand up for herself and let her actions speak for her.

I could trust her with anything big or small. She never needed to hear the same advice twice.

I missed her, too. I realised the feeling of lack of connection I had from missing her.

But now I'm happy; I'm no longer alone.

I found the teenage daredevil.

I'm the daredevil I was looking for.

YOUR LIFE WORK

1. This exercise is done with your eyes closed. Please read the instructions below before you do the exercise. You can have as many attempts as you like.

2. Think of an incident where you did something you later regretted – something minor, such as forgetting someone's birthday. Think of the incident and go back to when you realised you made a mistake and how you felt bad about yourself. Think about what you thought of yourself. Maybe you thought forgetting was bad, and you felt angry with yourself. Close your eyes and run through this scene in your mind. Pay attention to any physical sensations in your body. Do you feel tightness, pain or any other sensation?

   Next, acknowledge what led to you doing what you did exactly as it happened. Maybe you were too busy, maybe you were sick. Acknowledge that this happened for the reasons it happened. Understand your intentions from the previous version of you who made the mistake.

Then say silently: 'I'm so sorry, please forgive me, thank you, I forgive you, I forgive myself.' Hear those words in your voice and then hear the previous version of you saying that to you.

Once this is done, notice any changes to the sensations you feel in your body. Do you feel any lighter, as if you released something? Notice what is different.

3. Do this exercise every time you feel you are blaming yourself. For consistent results, start doing it daily at a convenient time – early in the morning, when you wake up, before you get out of bed, or before you go to sleep at night, whatever suits your lifestyle most.

4. Head over to **www.prowesscoaching.com.au** to download your free forgiveness meditation and start listening to it daily.

4

Live for today

*Live today as if it is the tomorrow
you would like to live.*

One simple truth is that you can never go back to yesterday or forward to tomorrow in advance. This truth shows the limits of our physical existence. We are here only today, only now.

Millions of cells in our bodies regenerate numerous times within a day; our physical bodies are reborn every fraction of a second. Similarly, our emotions and psychological state change every moment, and we are never the person we were a moment before. With every passing moment, there is a fresh start in a person's physical and mental state. The sad truth is that most of us like to hang onto the previous version of ourselves without acknowledging this constant state of starting all over again, which occurs naturally.

Today is the only day that matters; without it, there would be no tomorrow or yesterday. Unless you know how to time travel, you can only enjoy the present day and live in the present moment. What matters is how you can change what you think and do today, so that you do not face the same challenges you faced yesterday.

You could never have the same challenge you had yesterday because you are a new person today. All you can do is prepare for such a situation if you encounter one. The preparation that can be done today for a perceived future event is understanding what happened in the past without putting a label on it. As I have explained, when you label something, you stop seeing reality and only see a pattern you already know. In other words, when you stop being curious, you start being judgemental – about others or yourself.

Having a non-judgmental view of you and your surroundings gives you a fresh start on everyday events. Everyday events go on to make what we call life.

Being grateful for what you have and being able to forgive yourself and others for who they were in the past matters, as it allows you to embrace the new version of you born right now. Starting fresh does not mean you have to return to zero, as you could never return to the original starting point; you could only pick up from where you left off and consider matters from a fresh perspective. In the previous chapter, we discussed how negative emotions such as anger, fear, sadness, grief, shame and guilt leave you hooked on the past, preventing you from fully embracing the present moment. When that occurs, you operate from a previous version of yourself, which does not tally with what has happened since time has passed. Don't get me wrong; you need your emotions and to acknowledge their presence to make use of them. However, hanging onto them for extended periods, making others responsible for your emotions, or blaming yourself for doing what you did for the emotions to occur does not help.

A simple way of focusing on what matters now is to realise there is no tomorrow without today, and today is the only day you need to plan how to have the ideal tomorrow. You cannot find solutions to problems that are not there right now; you can only imagine what challenges may arise and be prepared to face them. If you are not preparing to face the challenges that might arise tomorrow, there is no point thinking about them, as it just makes you more fearful of doing what you need to do.

The real question is how are we supposed to live this day called 'today' or this moment called 'the present moment'? Others have asked me the same question, and I am curious about the answer.

There are two solution-oriented ways of approaching the problem: you can focus on how to live each moment, or you can focus on how you want to live each day. I suggest you learn both, as both are equally important.

How can you live in the present moment? How can you bring yourself into the present moment when you are distracted? To live in the present moment, you need to bring your attention one hundred per cent to *right now*. What you might experience in such a state is quietness in your head as you start to notice other sounds and activities in your surroundings. You will find yourself fully focused on whatever you do, but at the same time, you will notice what is going around you and not be distracted by it. You are then fully focused on the now. This relaxed state allows you to be open to learning new things and being connected to your surroundings.

People live in the present moment in their daily lives for varied lengths of time. Some people habitually do it for longer periods with the help of activities they have trained themselves to engage in.

Some people experience living in the present moment only randomly, while others live in the present moment by choice. The question is how to bring yourself back to the present moment when you are *not* in the present moment.

A simple way to be in the present moment is through connecting with nature and doing an activity that arouses your curiosity. These activities will likely vary from person to person; a few common examples are gardening, bushwalking or creative activities such as painting, drawing or dancing. You are in the 'now' when you engage in an activity that you fully enjoy and give your attention to one hundred per cent. It differs from doing an activity out of habit and getting lost in your head, entangled in thoughts, or staying focused on an activity while trying to shut down everything else completely.

As much as you are responsible for your life and the experiences you create, you are responsible for every moment you live. You must be mindful of what is happening with your focus and bring it back to where it should be in case you lose focus. No one can ever have their attention glued only to one thing; it would be a dangerous way to live. It is natural for the mind to wander, as it is how the mind works by default. Imagine what would happen if it were not, and you stayed stuck, focused only on one thing, and needed voluntary control to change your point of focus! The unconscious mind monitors what's happening around you and diverts your attention to what is important to your survival. That is the natural state. Spending most of your day focused only on what you are doing and ignoring what is going around you is, not surprisingly, tiring and a hyper-focused state driven by fear. You need to move your attention fully between tasks and changing demands. What you could do is to know the mind wanders and accept that fact, as it is the nature of the mind that ensures survival. Then you can bring your attention back to where it needs to be without fighting with yourself.

Incorporating activities that interest you and keep you curious in your daily life is a way of staying in the present moment for longer. You are more relaxed when you spend most of your time in your natural state. If you need to shut down what is happening around you completely to focus, it means you have difficulty staying focused. That can be because of many reasons outside this book's scope. I'm not talking about trying to meditate sitting beside a performing rock star. The more you can be aware of what is happening but focused enough to keep you curious and non-judgemental, the more you can live in the present moment. Remember the example of the red rose in chapter 1? A newborn with no pre-learned associations appreciates the red rose's presence and is curious about it, and wants to learn what it is. The newborn is fully present as they attempt to understand the red rose to the best of their ability.

Here is a simple exercise to bring your attention fully to the present moment.

> *Close your eyes while sitting comfortably, feet on the floor. Bring your attention to your breathing. Feel the breath entering and leaving your nostrils. Then, focus on how your chest and abdomen move with breathing.*

Extend your awareness to feel your body holding its posture. Feel your body against the surface you are sitting on. Feel your feet on the ground. Stay in this state as long as you can. You may notice that your breathing becomes slower and deeper while you feel more relaxed. You will notice a quietness in your head and the mental chatter disappearing.

Do this activity when you feel stressed or emotionally disturbed. The more you practise, the longer you can stay in this state. Make it into a habit.

If you have difficulty bringing yourself to the present state, you will benefit from a shift in your emotional state. That is explained further in chapter 5.

One thing that changed my life dramatically was that I started living today as if it were the tomorrow I expected. I started thinking about my desired version of myself and certain things as if I had all I wanted from the future. I understood I must be a different version of myself to do what I planned to do with my life. Since I was little, I dreamed of living in a big mansion; you read about that earlier in this book. I understood I had to do things differently and think differently to have this type of mansion for myself. I started thinking about how I would think if I owned one. That showed me the gap between how I *was* thinking and how I *would be* thinking if I already owned one. I started reducing the gap by actively thinking I already owned this mansion. For example, I thought about how I would maintain or decorate it. This simple exercise made me realise

I did not have the skills to maintain a mansion like that in the way I desired. The more I understood that, the more I realised most of what I expected from that mansion was within the house I already lived in. It was not the mansion I needed, but the skills to maintain it. It became apparent that I was so lost in my fantasy of the future, I had failed to realise I already had what I wanted. That shifted me to think of ways to improve my experience in the house I was living in rather than trying to build another. That exercise alone gave me many insights into why I was not living in a mansion. The problems I identified changed my whole life and how I lived it.

I realised I was still living in survival mode and running away from poverty. I had no plans for financial success or to earn wealth that allowed me to have the mansion I desired. Then, I realised I had to improve my financial knowledge and work on my money mindset. I understood that a person living in a multi-million dollar mansion would have a different attitude and beliefs about money than I did. The more I worked on those things, the more I realised the wealth I wanted was within my reach. I'd had the same amount of money for years, but still felt very poor. When I worked on my money mindset, my attitude towards money changed, and I could change certain things in my finances to the point that I did not feel poor anymore. Instead, I started to feel financially secure because of how I thought about money and what I did to ensure I was financially secure.

I used to dwell a lot on my past and future, which made me feel disconnected from the rest of the world. However, as I learned to let go of anger and practise forgiveness and gratitude, I began to see people without judgment and accept them for who they were. I realised it is not my responsibility to like or dislike others for their life choices. Instead, I should focus on living my life to the fullest. This understanding helped me connect with people who made me feel comfortable and let go or create a distance from those who didn't. As I became more connected with the people around me, it became easier to focus on the present and find solutions to problems rather than worry about the future. I learned to be content with my achievements and how I live today. I moved from wanting to finish a task to being happy with what I had done already.

Realising that I needed to know what to do with my life to live the present day with purpose made a massive change in my life and in how I do things. I understood that waking up without a plan for the day led me to spend most of my time dwelling on the past or worrying about the future, which made me unhappy. Although I had set some goals for my future, I was not acting towards achieving them with consistency. That made me take longer to achieve what I wanted. I was confused and overwhelmed by my goals, and I feared failure. So, I set clear goals where I had none before. I realised that a life vision helps a person create short-term goals and achieve them successfully, more effectively and with enthusiasm. Without a long-term goal or a vision for my life, I made small goals to help me survive and escape my fears.

When I decided what I wanted from my life and how I wanted to live, it was easy to decide what I wanted for the next ten years, five years and twelve months. Then, deciding what I wanted for one day became much easier. I struggled to have a daily routine for many years, preventing me from acting on my goals. This problem was solved instantly when I decided what I wanted from my life. I realised that success and a beautiful, exciting life would not come about accidentally, but would require conscious choices and ongoing attention and effort.

What stopped me from having a life goal was that I was running away from my fears, expecting that life would somehow bring me what I wanted, a belief that made me dependent on others for the life I wanted. It made me realise I was too afraid to wish for what I wanted from life because I believed it was impossible to have what I wanted.

I overcame the belief that I couldn't have what I wanted by understanding that we each perceive the world differently. I am responsible for creating my life the way I desire because I'm the only person who can do it the way I want. No one shares the interpretation I have of what is around me. I'm one unique being; this is the truth about each of us.

In a world that changes every moment, we – beings with a human body and a mind that changes every moment – go on a journey to destinations we either aim for or just end up, depending on the choices we make. We are free to see what we see, hear what we hear and feel what we feel because all our experiences are unique to us. What we see, hear and feel gives us the experience we call life. Life is completely our choice. If life is our choice, we can create any life we want. No one can ever give us permission to live the life we wish to live; it is futile to expect permission from others who cannot experience the life you experience.

Does the world really exist? Where are we? Where do we exist, and where is the universe located? If there is a location where the whole universe is located, what is that location? When I studied physics, they taught us that the visual images formed in the human eye are upside down. Does that mean the world we see is an upside-down version of what exists? Does that mean humans are upside down as they walk and do what they do? If everything around us changes every fraction of a second, and if we change every fraction of a second, and if people never perceive the same object the same way, do we really exist?

We interpret what is around us uniquely, depending on how each person's mind is set. We live in an illusion that can be interpreted in any way we like, based on our thoughts. We could make any choice, which would be granted because it originates from our unique mind. As we live, we create more and more illusions by choice. I see a different interpretation of my life from how I interpreted the same events ten years ago. I could interpret them differently, too; that would make me have a different life altogether.

You can interpret your world in any way you choose and live a different version of the same life based on your choices. You are born free to live how you like, in your natural state. The sad reality is that people create barriers around them, limiting their original capacity to live that life out of fear. The fear of failure, the fear of being different, the fear of being judged, the fear of being excluded, and so on.

None of those fears matter because they are based on futile concepts that do not exist.

There is no such thing as failure in a world that can be interpreted differently by choice; there are only experiences.

There is no such thing as being different, as we are all very different. There is only uniqueness that is common to everyone.

There is no judgment, only a unique point of view. What you see in others is what you are.

Exclusion does not exist in a world that does not exist. You are solo in your unique journey called life anyway. You can never be excluded from a place without inclusion.

What matters is what you do at any given time, knowing that moment never arrives again. There is no need to react, as what you experience is an illusion. You always have a choice on how to respond and behave.

How you respond and behave matters, as that decides your unique lifestyle.

According to Maslow's hierarchy of needs[1,2] humans have basic needs that can be described in five categories:

1. **Physiological needs** – biological needs for human survival such as food, shelter, water, breathing and sleep.

2. **Need for safety and security** – what people need to ensure order, predictability and control in their lives, such as health, employment, property, family and social ability.

3. **Need for love and belonging** – such as connectedness, interpersonal relationships and being part of a group.

4. **Self-esteem needs** – such as self-worth, accomplishment and respect.

5. **Self-actualisation needs** — including the realisation of potential, self-fulfilment, seeking personal growth, and peak experiences and performance.

This hierarchy forms a pyramidal structure, and according to this model, self-actualisation needs are at the highest end, and physiological needs are at the very broad, basic level. The basic needs must be fulfilled before those higher in the order are.

It is your responsibility to ensure those needs are met in your day-to-day life in an ecological way that suits you and your abilities. From a child dependent on an adult for survival to a multi-millionaire, everyone has the same basic needs. What differs is how you go about ensuring those needs are fulfilled. How you achieve them makes the difference in how you spend your day and how you live your life. How you respond to the challenges you perceive creates the lifestyle you live. There is always a choice, whether to provide a service to earn an income or to break the bank to be rich.

If you reflect on your life, you will realise that the drive for whatever you did or plan to do in the future is to ensure those needs are met. Your upbringing and actions in achieving your goals, your surroundings and the culture you relate to shape how those needs are met. As everyone's abilities vary physically and mentally, some people achieve those higher needs much more easily than others. Some can tolerate the effort required to achieve those needs longer and under dire circumstances, while others cannot.

That makes your life experience different from anyone else's. As I mentioned earlier, thoughts precede actions, and actions create experiences. Experiences create life. As any action begins in the mind before manifesting physically, what matters is how well-suited your thoughts are for the actions to be consistently effective and efficient in achieving those needs so that your day becomes enjoyable – and ultimately, your life becomes more enjoyable.

The more enjoyable thoughts you have, the more enjoyable actions you will have. The more enjoyable days you have, the more enjoyable life becomes.

If the future version of you behaves in a certain way to have that beautiful life you desire, you need to have those qualities today. If the future warrants you having a certain knowledge to live that life, you need that knowledge today. If you behave in a certain way in the future, you need to behave that way today. If there are activities you will do in the future, you need to be doing them today.

As I moved down this pathway, I realised I would do some things even if I became richer, anyway. I realised a certain lack in some areas; I started incorporating those that were lacking into my daily life. I like writing books. I started writing this book, and that experience brings me much joy. Would I be practising medicine if I had millions? I had asked that question many times before and realised I would be doing so. So that would stay, but it allowed me to decide when I would no longer be practising medicine. I liked to coach people, so I made my coaching calendar available and prepared for that in my schedule. I spend a lot of time with my family, but I would do that anyway, irrespective of my level of wealth. The more I incorporated the things I liked doing into my daily schedule, the more I realised there were things I would rather delegate. It helped me free my time for more things I enjoy. I like learning new knowledge and personal development, so I made time available for those areas.

If I were to die today, I would have accomplished everything I wanted to do in life. I understand that my expectations may change as I grow older, but at this moment, this is what I desire. I have no unfulfilled goals or loose ends to tie up when I pass away. For me, this is what fulfilment means.

When you live the present day with activities that create interest and joy in your life, why would you need holidays to rejuvenate?

I moved from a person craving holidays to someone who feels that staying home with my family is like a holiday. There was a time in my life when I would plan holidays, as I felt emotionally stressed, disconnected and isolated. Then I realised that those feelings do not go away by having holidays. I would return from holiday feeling more isolated and disconnected. The more I connected with myself and the people who mattered to me, the more I realised I needed to stay home when I had those feelings so I could connect with the people that matter. For me, that is my biggest achievement in life.

Similarly, you have a choice in behaving the way that feels right for you. How you behave is who you are. How you see others is also who you are.

Therefore, your only choice is to ensure your internal world is like the external world you wish to experience, because your external world is a representation of your internal world.

If you want others to be kind to you, you must be kind to others.

If you want to live longer, ensure you harm no living being.

If you wish to hear kind words, speak kind words.

What you receive is what you give.

What you see, hear and feel are what you do to others.

You attract what you already are, not what you want. If you want what you want, you must make an internal change to be what you want first in your inner state.

You cannot change the external world without changing the internal world first.

If you want to live a beautiful and exciting life, create that life in your mind. The world you create in your mind is the world you experience. That happens whether you are aware of it or not. If you want to live a particular lifestyle, be the person in that lifestyle now.

If you want to be happy, be happy now. Be happy with what you have right now.

If you want to be rich, be a rich person now. Some people report feeling very poor even when they have millions. Be a person who feels truly wealthy and has habits of wealth that attract riches to them. A person can earn millions and have debts over a few million. It is up to you to decide how you define wealth.

If you want a good family life with lots of loving connections, have the connections now and work on them to make you available to your family today, not in ten years when you have finished all your projects.

The life you want to live is for you to create; no one can tell you how you want to live. Accordingly, no one can create it for you – only you can.

What you believe about yourself shapes who you are. Your beliefs influence the people you surround yourself with, and you learn from those relationships. Your current life reflects your upbringing, social circle and past experiences. You may feel disconnected from some of your connections as you grow and change, but this is natural. You will create new connections, which may differ from your previous ones. You may even develop a deeper understanding of people you already know.

After all, everyone comes into this world alone, even if they are surrounded by family watching their birth. Until we connect with others, we are strangers struggling to understand where and what we are doing. When someone dies, they leave everything and everyone else behind, embarking on a lonely journey. A famous saying goes, 'How it starts is how it finishes', and I see that theme throughout life. We are born alone, and we die alone. In between birth and death, we live in our interpretation of the world, surrounded by others in our physical reality, but ultimately, we are one unique being, having a solo trip from birth to death. To me, a life means one spiritual being in transit from birth to death, dancing to the tune of one's inner self. All we can do is update our song so that this transit is smoother and with minimal conflict with those around us.

If you want to live a life without regrets, you must accept that there are no mistakes or failures, only experiences. However, it's important to remember that this does not permit anyone to engage in criminal activities. We must respect the rules and regulations of society and set boundaries for ourselves, while also respecting the boundaries of others.

Once I realised the truth about life, I reconditioned my brain for success and gave up self-blaming and regret. I embarked on self-discovery, learning new skills and even writing a book.

Reflecting on my life, what I once perceived as a mistake was a detour that provided me with additional skills to utilise in the future. Despite the ups and downs, I still maintain the same level of enthusiasm and joy for life that I had as a child. I am living the life that I desire.

By committing to ongoing personal development, you can work on the challenges you face today. No one can address problems that have not yet arisen, so the best way to improve your present situation is to work on the issues you currently face. This will help make your day better.

What does personal development mean to you?

Personal development refers to the process of self-improvement, which enables us to enhance our capacity as human beings in various aspects of our lives. It involves upskilling in different areas to help us better interact with others and live our lives to our fullest potential mentally. Personal development is a continuous process that never ends and evolves with the person.

There is a Chinese proverb that says, 'When the winds of change blow. Some people build walls. Others build windmills.'

Personal development allows you to build windmills when life winds blow. The windmill does not change the winds but uses the wind and its power to create something that would benefit both the person building the windmill and many others.

Personal development intends that you change internally in the face of external events to improve your capacity to face such events. Remember, we are in connection with all living beings and the environment we live in. When we change, others change inevitably.

As Lord Buddha famously said, 'Change is the only thing that does not change.' Today, quantum theories have shown that the world and the universe are made of small particles that change and move constantly. We are largely made of space that changes its shape and size constantly. The person changes with every moment, making each encounter unique.

Friendships fall apart over disagreements, marriages break down over changing hearts, and businesses are bankrupted over investors pulling out. When one thing changes, other things that do not change offer resistance. Resisting change causes pain.

A person told me she would not let her ex-husband get away from her, so she kept rejecting a divorce. They were high-school sweethearts, and once they had finished their higher education, they got married. Soon after the marriage, her husband found a new love relationship with one of his workmates and wanted to separate from his wife. The wife kept rejecting the divorce so that he could not get away from her, even though she understood that he no longer enjoyed her company and had had a change of heart. Her revenge was the divorce papers she refused to sign so that the new partner did not get to marry her ex-husband.

Does causing pain for another relieve an aching heart? Her husband had moved on; she was still in the same old place. Her ex-husband and his new partner decided they did not want to marry but to live together and form a family. The woman could not stop that process, as she did not have control over the matter. All she had control over was her own life. What would her life be like today if she had moved on? I wonder.

It's crucial to acknowledge the changes in our lives, even if they are unwanted. Change is inevitable, and resisting it can cause pain and discomfort, just like the woman did when she carried hatred and wanted revenge. She was stuck, unable to forgive and move on. But the more we struggle to accept change, the more we suffer. It's best to welcome change and find ways to adapt which benefit us and those around us. Engaging in personal development and growth can help us navigate change with grace and fulfilment. The husband changed internally when he decided on a different path in his life and abandoned a fight with his ex-wife over the unsigned divorce papers. He found a way to his happiness. The wife found a way to long-lasting agony, through intending to create agony for another.

Could she have found a trustworthy relationship and a happy life if she had let the husband get a divorce and moved on with her life? After all, her high school sweetheart was clearly not the best match for her – otherwise, they could have continued for longer together like they promised each other.

With her husband leaving her, she had an opportunity to find another person to suit her and the future she wanted to have. Surely, there are enough men and women around for each of us to find a good relationship. But, in her state of agony and hatred, she could not see the opportunity for a better life. After all, why would you want to hold on to someone you could not trust?

Resisting change comes from a fear of inadequacy. The universe is abundant, and the illusion of the life we create lets us have what we want without depriving another.

Through personal development, you can create a win-win situation by interpreting what you define as failure differently.

Forgiveness is critical to success. Successful people forgive themselves and others quickly and move forward. They take personal development seriously and make it a part of their daily routine by regularly engaging in coaching and other personal growth activities.

Just imagine how freeing it would be to forgive and let go of past events, allowing you to move forward easily in your everyday life. Personal development helps you to forgive yourself for any mistakes you may have made and move on. This also allows you to extend forgiveness to others, as everything starts with you. As I have explained previously, what you perceive as external is your internal state. You forgive yourself and others; you find others forgiving you.

To move forward in life, you must practise forgiveness regularly; it's best to incorporate that into your daily life and form a routine around it, as I mentioned in chapter 3.

If you find yourself stuck and unable to progress towards your goals, a qualified coach can help you break free and identify the areas where you may be unintentionally hindering your success or causing stress in your daily life. Alternatively, you can read self-help books and participate in programs to learn and grow independently. However, this approach may take a long time and may only be effective if you find the right resources to work with. In today's world, there are more options than ever before for personal development.

Life is simple. You only need to deal with one person your whole life. Even better – that person is you. Whether you have lived a hundred years or more, you must only deal with one day at a time. All you need to ensure is that you live that day with joy and fulfilment, creating a fulfilled past and future as you move along.

Personal development is the pathway to change – creating a happy life with changing demands over time. Personal development is how you grow into the life you intend to live without needing to stop, rejuvenate and fill the tank. When your life is about doing what you really want to do from the bottom of your heart, and growing as a person to meet the demands of those desires, there is nothing to balance. Then you get to enjoy what you do every day. And what you do is what you call life.

YOUR LIFE WORK

Reflect on the goal you wrote down at the end of chapter 2.

Think of a day in your ideal life in the following terms:

- What makes you feel safe emotionally, physically and financially? Have you included that in your day?

- Have you included time for connection and fulfilling relationships in your daily routine?

- Do you have time for self-care in your day?

- What defines fun for you? How do you include that in your day?

- Do you have activities that stretch your imagination and consciousness? If your goal seems achievable, there is no space for growth there. Your goal needs to help you grow beyond your comfort zone.

- Do you have a vision and activities to serve others as you grow?

5

Let nature take over your pain

Be prepared to leave with no prior notice.

How would I do what I do if I knew it was my last day on earth? This is a question I have asked myself over and over. By now, I'm well trained to think more deeply on this topic to find the direction I need to take in life.

When I leave this world, I want to feel satisfied and grateful for my life and excited about where I'm going. I would like to leave a legacy behind so that others can continue my business.

The question is, as death can come without warning, how am I to make sure that, when I die, I leave in a satisfied and grateful state? I must know how to be in that state every day. It would be wonderful to feel like that every day anyway, irrespective of impending death.

Death is inevitable. We are born ready to die. We all change at a quantum level every fraction of a second; therefore, it could be considered that we are dying and being reborn with each passing moment. That is our natural state. However, at a conscious level, the thought of death brings fear and anxiety as we love our lives and live hanging on to the very last moment of what we cherish.

When I was younger, I used to wish that I would die in my sleep so that I would not be aware of what was happening. With maturity and knowledge, I now see that thinking about the last moments of my life has helped me immensely in how I live every day and interact with others.

What if I died while screaming at my child because they did something I disapproved of?

How would they remember their last interaction with their mother?

She was screaming and controlling even when she died. She wasn't happy at her death, just like always.

Is that how I want to be remembered?

No.

If people remember me after I die, I would like them to have happy, loving memories about me. That thought shifted me to change my responses to everyday events and dig deep into patterns of behaviour hardwired into my brain.

Learning to quickly shift your emotional state is a powerful skill for changing your life so that you can learn to break those patterns of behaviour. There are simple and quick ways to change your emotional state so that you respond to situations rather than reacting. If you want to learn more, head over to **www.prowesscoaching.com.au** to download a free resource on how to change your emotional state quickly.

Death is instantaneous and may even come without warning.

Knowing that death can come at any point in time made me realise I needed to do things differently and gave me insight into what I needed to prioritise in my life. The things that take priority in my life are the ones I prioritise in my day, as my day is my life. It shifted my thinking to a whole new level about how I plan my future, businesses and relationships.

How do I ensure I'm always fulfilled and not in a state of desire or craving anymore? If I'm craving more, even at the time of my death, I could still be unhappy to leave. I understand that lasting happiness comes from within. The only thing I can be happy about is myself. How do I ensure I'm always happy from within and not punishing myself?

Feeling grateful keeps you happy and satisfied. Because life is a continuum, what is enough now may be seen as insufficient in the future; you can only be grateful for what you have enjoyed. Craving for something can come due to a feeling of lack, but if you stay in the present moment and are grateful for what you have, craving can be reduced.

How do I not crave but still earn profits in what I do?

Money is energy. Money comes and goes as you give and receive. Craving comes from feeling a need for wealth. You crave when you stop receiving. You stop craving when you allow yourself to receive. Receiving is not just money going into your bank account – receiving is enjoying your wealth and using it to uplift your existence. When you allow yourself to receive and accept wealth and enjoy what you have, you facilitate energy flow, and nothing is lost. To stay in the loop of giving and receiving, you need to believe you deserve the profit you receive in exchange for the service you provide.

I don't crave the mansion with high ceilings and lavender anymore. That was a massive relief for me. I'm happy with where I live right now. I'm grateful I have a roof over my head with no debts. So, when I leave here, I won't leave a debt for my family to repay on my behalf. Instead, I will leave them financially stable and with a roof over their heads. With that, I feel very wealthy. I still like mansions, but it doesn't pressure me anymore. I can think of moving to a bigger space when I need more space. I don't need a mansion to help me shine. Instead, I help the place I live in now to shine because that is where I live.

Right now, I'm too busy living my exciting life and creating the legacy I will leave behind.

I feel very light and relaxed in my heart. I have no pressure to achieve any more. I'm already doing what I like to do. What matters in life is not what you want to achieve, but how you live that process until you achieve it.

I help children learn with my expertise in paediatrics. I help people change their lives for the better with my coaching. I write, which keeps me calm and focused. I speak without fear and express and teach people what I know. I connect with people I love regularly. I sleep well, eat healthy and live healthy. I do what I like from morning till evening and continue that the next day. Most importantly, I'm happy with myself.

I feel sad for my dear friend who took his own life. Would he have done that if he knew life could be changed?

There are various speculations about life after death, mostly associated with religions. Some believe we are born again and again, while others believe we are never born again. Some religions speak about heaven or hell that we return to, while others don't. How much does modern-day science tell us about what happens after death?

My understanding of what happens after death comes from Buddhism, which describes a cycle of life and death all humans, animals and other living forms experience.

Buddha also explains how an exit from this vicious cycle of life and death can be attained through a higher level of consciousness. In that context, the way to exit an agonising life is not via death, but by living at a higher level of consciousness. Life was meant to be lived with ease and fulfillment at a higher level of consciousness. From a life coach's perspective, a higher level of consciousness can be achieved by knowing how to deal with negative emotional states, practising forgiveness, gratitude and understanding, and removing the mental frames we impose on ourselves. That is where personal development comes in and can help us create a much more pleasurable life. Personal development helps people live at a higher level of consciousness.

The events that occur at death have no transit time. According to Buddha, you leave one side to be in another in a fraction of a second, and the spiritual energy continues in a different form. Buddha explains this with the example of lighting a candle using another that is already lit. The candle that was already lit had its flame. And then gave birth to a second flame on another candle. Both flames exist at the same time. Nothing is lost; so I understand that the spiritual being, or energy, continues to be unstoppable, even after death.

The energy exists in a different form even if you kill your physical body to escape suffering. To end suffering, you must end existence. There is no real you, as the energy represents you and others. You cannot kill something that does not exist – you cannot kill what *you* call yourself because it does not exist. What you call yourself changes constantly, so new versions of you are born every moment. Which version would someone kill if they must kill themselves?

It is said our emotions and mental state in the very last moment decide where we are born in the next lifetime. If you are not from a Buddhist background and do not believe in rebirth, you may find this difficult to comprehend. In the personal development world, it is considered that how you start something is how you end it. If you start a journey feeling unhappy, you will have an unhappy journey. Death can be seen as an end from one perspective and a start from another.

One skill that can help you prepare for the unexpected is learning to change and shift your emotional state quickly. There are simple techniques to shift your emotional state that you can use anytime. People naturally feel anger, fear, sadness, guilt, shame and grief at times, but learning to express those emotions is a resourceful skill everyone needs. You could leave an unpleasant situation emotionally if you cannot leave it physically. First, you must shift your mental and emotional state to respond to the situation appropriately. It all starts with the thought of changing – a *decision* to change. If you have decided to change your life, reviewing how you respond to changes in your emotional state would be a useful practice. If you need further information on this skill, head to www.prowesscoaching.com.au and download the free resource on how to quickly change your emotions in a hurry.

There was a lot of speculation about the death of my friend who took his own life, but no one ever knew why he did it – and no one could ever know. No one shares another person's agony or pain, or the details of another person's interpretation of the world if it was not shared, and it can never be fully shared. Is there a way to leave an agonising life and be re-born in a better life without leaving this physical existence?

Yes, there is.

A person does not have to kill themselves to start a new life and they don't need to learn how to end their spiritual existence, either.

As already mentioned, we are re-born every fraction of a second. The future and the past do not exist. The present creates the past. You can always leave an agonising life at any moment and start afresh. That is how you could let nature take over your pain – by grasping the opportunity to be reborn as a new person while still living. Deciding to be grateful for who you are while you forgive yourself and others is all that you need to start anew.

Suicide is running away from life. Instead of running away from the life you do not want, you could aim to live a life that excites you. There is an opportunity to do that every fraction of a second.

A spiritual being needs a physical body and an abstract mind to exist on Earth. You are not your body or your mind; you cannot cure your painful mind by killing your physical body. Do we know enough about life after death to say it is better to die than to live? What if it is worse after death?

What you give others is what you receive.

—Sinhalese proverb

Your life is a mirror that tells you what you are right now. If you wish others to change so that your experiences improve, you must make that change yourself first. In other words, if you need to change your life, you must change who you are internally and embody those changes. The internal changes precede the external manifestations.

Ending your life may seem like a solution, but it is not, because if your life is so bad you feel like ending it, this means you have not lived a life that feels good to you. You cannot quit something you are yet to start. What you can do instead is end the old life of hardship and start a new life – the good life you deserve. You can end an emotionally drained and exhausted life any time you wish and start living a life that fills you with happiness and excitement.

Death used to be my plan B in most circumstances in life where I felt pressured to accept an outcome I did not want. For me, everything was either do or die. If I cannot do it, I die. But I did not want to die either. Reflecting on the past, I understand how a person might feel when they live in survival mode for a long time. Death becomes an option when there is no solution to the challenges faced, and the person lives in fear, by default.

But in reality, there is always a solution to every challenge faced. But, unless you understand your struggle and accept that there is a solution to the situation that creates a problem for you, you will not see a solution.

If you have considered death as a solution to a problem, I must tell you this. After all my detours in my journey through life, I understood that if something feels so difficult, I'm doing it wrong. This is a principle I follow and have proven to be true over the years with what I have achieved.

If life feels difficult, you are living it wrong. Only you can correct it.

Think of the example of the red rose in chapter 1. Life is an illusion – we interpret it through what we already know. As we all live the illusion of life, we can interpret the illusion in a way that feels good for us. We draw our destiny out of an illusion that allows us to create whatever we want based on our thoughts. That allows us to have enough of what we want without depriving another. Because we operate from our interpretation of what we experience, it is possible to have what we want and not deprive another. In that space of abundance where you can ask for whatever you want and have whatever you ask for, there is unlimited potential for a new start.

As your thoughts precede your actions, you can leave your life and start another just with the thought of letting go and re-starting. It's possible to leave an agonisingly exhausting life and start another in a fraction of a second because that is what happens naturally anyway in our physical and emotional reality, although we are not consciously aware of it. You need to decide what you want to do and do it. Just like your old pattern of thoughts gave you an agonisingly exhausting life, your new pattern of thoughts can give you a happy and exciting life.

Imagine if you could restart your life and not have the agony and exhaustion: what would your life be like then? What would your life be if you had everything you wanted and lived up to your ultimate potential as a human being with no restrictions on how you express yourself and the energy that flows through you? Would you like to leave that kind of life ever? I doubt you would.

But death is something all of us will undoubtedly face – the end to our physical existence. We are born destined to die and experience the ultimate goodbye.

How would you live your life in a way that would lead you to accept death with grace and know you have enjoyed your life to the fullest? You would learn to respond to situations, not react. To do this, you would need to be non-judgemental of yourself and others. By now, you know when people react to a situation, they are in survival mode, running away from life.

Life becomes tolerable when you remove judgements you impose upon yourself and others. You don't need to run away from a tolerable life.

Death is not a new experience for anyone. It is a familiar and regular experience that is unappreciated because most people do not understand the reality of it. You don't have to waste your time killing yourself – it happens naturally. At a quantum level, there is a version of you that dies and a new version of you born every moment. As Buddha famously said, you do not meet the same person twice. That is because the person has changed within a fraction of a second, and you also change within that timeframe. So every encounter is a new one, although to the naked eye it is not. This continues throughout our journey from birth to death in our physical and emotional reality. Most of us understand birth and death, but dying and rebirthing these new versions of ourselves, which happens throughout our lives without being visible to the naked eye, is unappreciated because of the very nature of it. You need to accept and mentally allow the re-birthing process that happens naturally every moment, so that you can move on with your new life happily with the understanding the past cannot be changed.

Trying to kill yourself is futile. There have been many versions of yourself that have died and many versions of yourself that have been born at a quantum level until now. The one who decided on the suicide and the one who carries out the plan to die are different versions; and the one who is reading this book is not the same as the one who would finish reading this book because you change so much, so fast. It is a continuous process common to all of us. Which version of you are you killing, if you must?

If you are thinking of suicide, you have not lived life. If you live your life to the fullest, you won't feel a need to kill yourself. You cannot kill a life you haven't lived.

Life is a process of non-ending goal setting and leaving without the goals being complete. Because you change so fast at a quantum level, the version that completed the goal is not the version who set the goal. There is no point getting frustrated with what you could not have or could not achieve. You can only do your best at any given moment and be satisfied with what you have done, because in the next moment it will a new you who would pick up from where you finished in your previous version. So there is always a new beginning, a new start and a new opportunity to do better.

Life becomes easy when you understand you change every fraction of a second physically and emotionally, as does everyone else. There is only one thing that is permanent, and that is, according to Buddha, the process of change we all undergo. Nothing else is permanent. All living beings and non-living materials undergo change. People grow older and die. That is a natural process. For that process to happen, we change constantly at a quantum level not visible to the naked eye. We get to see the fine lines that appear in our skin, the changing body shape, the grey hair – but we do not see them until they are apparent to the naked eye; we do not see how they occur at a quantum level. Death is inevitable, as that is where we have been heading since the moment we were born. You are born destined to die. But the moment of your death may come with no warning.

The more I understood this, the more relaxed I felt. I understood I needed to live prepared to welcome the sudden arrival of death at any moment. With this understanding, I now do everything with a different perspective – how do I leave suddenly and not be upset, but be excited because I have lived my beautiful, exciting life? A happy life does not have to have an unhappy end. So how do I leave this world excited about where I'm going after death?

If I knew I was going to a nice place after death, would I be feeling upset or excited?

Do I know where I'm going after death? No.

How can I be excited at death not knowing where I'm going?

By living in the present moment. You do not know what is coming in the next moment, although you may wish you knew what was coming. But what you don't know, you don't know.

Let nature take over your pain

You can only live *right now*. In the next fraction of a second, you will change to be a different version again.

So if you are happy and excited *right now*, that is what matters. If you live happily in each moment, you will leave happily.

The more you can enjoy the process of non-ending goal setting, knowing that you actually won't achieve what you would like to achieve because it is a new you who achieves the goal set by an older version of you, and also knowing you will not necessarily have another shot at completing your goal because you might not be alive in the next moment, the easier life is to tolerate and the happier it is. With the constant changes that occur at a quantum level and the death that marks the end of life, the only choice you have is to understand that you never complete what you start and to accept it, as that is not something you can change.

Knowing that end of life is inevitable at any moment, how would you do what you do every day, if you knew it was your last chance to do what you do?

How would you speak with a person, if it was your last time doing so? How would you do your business deals if it was the last thing you did before you died? What things would you think of, if it was your last moment on earth? Because, in reality, it is always your last chance in everything you do. You get so many chances to do your best every moment, because you are a different version afterwards at a quantum level and there is a new you, re-starting each moment.

Life is about learning to achieve, losing with grace, and being happy with how far you have come. You could do your best at any time and be happy because you know you won't get another opportunity to do your best in that situation again. The lost opportunity never comes back, but then there is a new opportunity waiting to be embraced. If you miss that opportunity, don't worry, there will be another and another until you die. Forgiving yourself for what you could not do and forgiving others for not meeting your expectations helps you embrace the present moment and embrace the new opportunity that has arrived. You only need to deal with one moment, and that is the present moment.

If you do not forgive yourself, why would others forgive you? You need to forgive yourself for others to follow your lead and forgive you. Forgiveness is the key to winning any situation. If you want to win the game of life, you need to learn to forgive.

Do you also watch tennis, like I do?

The Australian Open is a big event I look forward to in the summer. I always thought it was easy to predict the person who would win the match by observing how they behave when things are tough. The person who breaks racquets and argues with the umpire often seems to be losing. Their body language reflects their level of performance and their level of belief in themselves. The player who wins does what they must do, no matter what. The frustrated player is the one not doing their best; if they were doing their best, there would be nothing to get frustrated about.

If life is frustrating, you are not doing your best. Your best is what you can do right now. There is no point in punishing yourself for not being better. Just do what you can and be grateful for what you did because you will invariably get another opportunity to do better and pick up from where you left off – if you are still alive.

Let nature take over your pain

In tennis, the players who do not trust in themselves are the ones who lose. It is the same in life.

If you do not trust yourself, why would others trust you? Trusting yourself is the ultimate self-love.

If you do not love yourself, why would others love you?

Life is simple. If it feels complicated, you are living it wrong. The only person you ever need to deal with is yourself. If dealing with yourself for a lifetime is too complicated, you could always focus on how to deal with yourself one day at a time. That becomes easier if you only focus on what is most important now.

Your life mirrors your internal state. To receive love, you must start loving yourself. It's never too late to start. You can start right now; there is an opportunity for a new start right now, this moment. Now is the right time to start all over again. Do it now.

YOUR LIFE WORK

1. What things have you always wanted to do and not had the opportunity to do?

2. Who do you want to be and have never had the opportunity to be?

3. What things have you always wanted to have and have never had?

4. How would you plan your future if you only had twenty years to live – what would do and who would you be? Consider the following areas of life:

- health and fitness
- work or business
- relationships with family and people that matter to you
- money and finances.

5. How would you plan your future if you knew you only had *one* year to live – what would do and who would you be? Consider the following areas of life:

    - health and fitness
    - work or business
    - relationships with family and people that matter to you
    - money and finances.

6. What would you prioritise in your day if you had one day to live? What things would you do differently? Consider the following areas of life:

    - health and fitness
    - work or business
    - relationships with family and people that matter to you
    - money and finances.

Afterword

Life is always simple when you operate from knowing that only you can create the life you desire. No one else can change your life for you. The biggest game changer in my life was connecting with my heart's desire to create a much bigger life than I could ever imagine. Hence, I developed the boldness and courage I needed to be that person, as well as experiencing the loneliness I sometimes feel in creating that life.

We are on a solo trip from birth to death, and it is our duty to make that journey smooth, joyful and enjoyable for ourselves. You do not need another person's permission to live the life you would like to live, and no one can ever give you permission, as they do not have the same vision you have for yourself.

You are never too late to refresh and restart, and you get countless opportunities to do this during your life – in fact, as many as you like.

There is no absolute end to anything as we all evolve and change with the never-changing rule of the universe – change. Change is constant and is common to all of us. We change at a quantum level every fraction of a second and that process continues throughout life. Life is a process of constant change, physically and emotionally. Change is the truth we must embrace as we live, and the more we are prepared to accept change, the smoother and easier our lives will be.

Life is simple. We only need to do one thing as long as we live. That is to live a fulfilling and happy life. That life can be defined as fulfilling and happy on many levels, as life unfolds with the creator. It's up to you to define your own level of fulfilment and your own level of happiness.

You are the creator. You create your life with the energy you infuse into your thoughts.

> *With our thoughts, we make the world.*
>
> —Buddha

***

'Mummy!'

Two little arms embrace me, and I feel the sudden, smooth hug stopping me from moving forward.

'So, mummy, why did you want to be a doctor?' asks Senuki.

'Because I like being one,' I reply.

'But, mummy, don't you ever get bored doing the same thing? I mean, you see your patients *every day!*' She rolls her eyes to emphasise her point.

Who taught you all these questions, Senuki? I wonder to myself, suppressing my laugh.

'No,' I say, 'because I can still do many things I like to do while seeing my patients. I get to switch roles and still be the doctor.'

'I want to be a doctor when I grow up, and also a teacher and a songwriter.'

'You always want to do a lot of things. Can you do one thing?' I hear Nisini voicing her opinions. *Where is she, and what is she doing?* I sweep the surroundings with my eyes, looking for her.

'Where is your sister?' I ask.

'Here!'

I see her beautiful face as she emerges from hiding to wrap her long arms and legs around me. She has the perfect eyes and the most beautiful smile I have ever seen in a five-year-old, radiating calmness and her quiet nature. Her fair skin feels velvety and cool against mine. *She is going to be tall and slim when she grows up.*

'You are the best mommy I could think of ... I never want you to die!' Senuki hugs me again. Her eyes twinkle as she speaks, as she looks into mine.

I hug both of them. We laugh as I tickle them, and they start looking for places to hide.

I'm at home. I'm living my life, happily ever after.

Endnotes

[1] Maslow, Abraham H. *(1943)*. 'A theory of human motivation'. *Psychological Review.* **50** *(4): 370–396.* CiteSeerX 10.1.1.334.7586. doi:10.1037/h0054346. hdl:10983/23610. ISSN 0033-295X. OCLC 1318836. Archived *from the original on September 14, 2017.* Retrieved March 13, 2007 – *via psychclassics.yorku.ca.*

[2] McCleod, S. A. (2018, May 21). *Maslow's hierarchy of needs.* Retrieved from https://www.simplypsychology.org/maslow.html

About the Author

When author **Dr Lakshinie Gunasiri** left Sri Lanka where she was born and raised and moved to Australia to find a new home, she faced all sorts of new challenges. She realised she would need to be a different version of herself to create the life she had always wanted. In pulling the pieces of that new version together, she embarked on a journey to rediscover herself, the strategies for which she shares in this book.

Dr Lakshinie is a multi-faceted professional with a lifelong curiosity for personal development and growth. She is a paediatrician and coach who has acquired many qualifications along the way, including neuro-linguistic programming and hypnosis at a mastery level, which she integrates into her work.

She believes personal empowerment is the key to success and advocates for creating ultimate holistic and harmonious growth in individuals to find a lifestyle that suits them.

Follow Dr Lakshinie Gunasiri on socials:

- **LinkedIn:** Lakshinie Gunasiri
- **Facebook:** Dr Lakshinie Gunasiri
- **Instagram:** @drlakshiniegunasiri

www.prowesscoaching.com.au

Acknowledgments

My heartfelt thanks go to everyone who helped me bring this book to life.

Chami, I love you. Thank you for letting me grow at my own pace in life and for all your words of encouragement and unwavering support.

Senuki and Nisini, thank you for enjoying the process of writing this book as much as I did. You inspire me.

Saroja, Nimashi and Gagani, thank you for taking the time to go through the manuscript and giving me your valuable insights.

All the coaches and counsellors who helped me be my best, thank you for helping me create the life I share in this book.

My mom & dad, all the teachers I've ever had – thank you.

I sincerely thank everyone who has inspired and encouraged me, and showed me love.

www.ingramcontent.com/pod-product-compliance
Lightning Source LLC
Chambersburg PA
CBHW050829160426
43192CB00010B/1948